a comprehensive
resource for traditional
country dancing

WHY DANCE?

jane downes MA and pat king

Foreword by Shirley Collins MBE, President, EFDSS

complete with two zesty
CDs of **dance length music**
courtesy of the catsfield steamers

Copyright © 2009 ~ Jane Downes MA and Pat King

www.whydance.org.uk

Published by Japacow Publishing, England

All rights reserved

No part of this publication may be reproduced, stored in a retrieval system, or transmitted in any form or by any means, electronic, mechanical, photocopying, recording or otherwise, without prior permission of Japacow Publishing.

A record of this publication is available from the British Library

ISBN 978-0-9561242-0-3

Printed in the United Kingdom by Hastings Print TN38 9BJ
www.hastings-print.co.uk

TRADITIONAL COUNTRY DANCE AND MUSIC

FOR

**FUN
HEALTH
EXERCISE
CO-ORDINATION
HIGH SELF ESTEEM**

WHY DANCE?

FOR

**YOUNG AND OLD

NEW OR ESTABLISHED DANCE CLUBS
TEACHERS & SUPPORT STAFF
PTA FUNDRAISERS
FAMILY DANCE CLUBS
YOUTH ORGANISATIONS
CHURCH GROUPS
OVERSEAS & EX-PAT DANCE GROUPS**

KEEPING OUR HERITAGE ALIVE

DEDICATION

We dedicate this WHY DANCE? pack with happy thanks to all the dancers and musicians we have worked with over the years.

Jane Downes MA and Pat King
January 2009

ACKNOWLEDGEMENTS

We would like to thank the following: the country dance band The Amazing Catsfield Steamers, Edd Blakeley, Will Downes for his wise advice, our proof readers and all those involved in project trials. Our especial thanks go to Colin King for his patient, professional and artistic working up of our text to produce Why Dance?

We owe a debt to the work of these callers:

Eddie Upton, Dave Hunt, Roger Watson, Fee Lock, Dave Roberts, Rachel Roberts, Vic Smith, Pat Shaw, Pete Collins, Dick Playll, Roy Dommett, Hugh Ripon, Tony Dunn, Gordon Potts, Nick Walden
and to the influence of
Ashley Hutchings, Vic Gammon and Shirley Collins.

Contents

Foreword

Introduction ~ Page 1

The Music ~ Page 2

The Dance ~ Page 3

Fitting the Dance to the Music ~ Page 4

Types of Tunes ~ Page 5

Dance with Children, and the Curriculum ~ Page 6

Dance with Adults ~ Page 8

Putting on a Dance ~ Page 8

Bibliography ~ Page 10

Track and Tune List ~ Page 11

Dance Notations

CD 1 / Track 1 ~ Page 12

CD 1 / Track 2 ~ Page 14

CD 1 / Track 3 ~ Page 17

CD 1 / Track 4 ~ Page 19

CD 1 / Track 5 ~ Page 21

CD 1 / Track 6 ~ Page 23

CD 1 / Track 7 ~ Page 25

CD 1 / Track 8 ~ Page 27

CD 2 / Track 1 ~ Page 29

CD 2 / Track 2 ~ Page 31

CD 2 / Track 3 ~ Page 33

CD 2 / Track 4 ~ Page 36

CD 2 / Track 5 ~ Page 38

CD 2 / Track 6 ~ Page 40

CD 2 / Track 7 ~ Page 43

Glossary ~ Page 45

Suggested Programmes for Beginners ~ Page 49

Or Experts ~ Page 49

Dance List ~ Page 50

FOREWORD

by Shirley Collins MBE, President, EFDSS

There was a time, as far back as the sixteenth century, when we were known throughout Europe as 'The Dancing English'. This excellent book will, I hope, help towards restoring that reputation!

Apart from the sheer pleasure of social dancing, the benefits are many. Everyone can join in; you don't need to be an expert, as the caller is there to talk you through the dance. Since country dancing is done in sets or circles, it's a social activity, a gathering of people that can embrace all age groups, and brings with it a sense of togetherness that, to my mind, we sorely need nowadays. It's also a healthy and entertaining way to exercise; older people can dance - perhaps more sedately than they once did - youngsters can learn co-ordination while letting off steam, and everyone can relish the simple delight, the good nature and the sweet innocence of a country dance.

WHY DANCE? comes complete with CDs of great dance-length tunes played by one of the very best bands - The Catsfield Steamers - music that will have you out of your seat and onto the dance floor.

So the main question is not – WHY DANCE? but WHY NOT?

Shirley Collins
Lewes ~ December 2008

INTRODUCTION

Country dance, barn dancing, traditional dance, social dance. Call it what you will, it should, above all else, be enjoyable. This, to us, is the core of all the dance activities we have ever undertaken.

Consider the history of world-wide social dance traditions. What do we find? Exuberance, joy, rhythm, elements of self expression, physical challenge.

People say of dances:

> 'Wicked, when are you coming again ?!..'

> 'What a relaxed, happy, jolly atmosphere...'

> 'When the music and dance entertains little ones, teenagers, and right through to our OAPs - that's really well done...'

> 'Time just flashed by, and everyone commented on the choice and quality of the music...'

> 'Completely forgot my wretched week...'

'Wellbeing in the 21st Century: an Enquiry into the Nation's Health', organised by the philanthropic Wellcome Trust in 2007, remarks on the potency of music and dance. 'Starting with the rhythm of your mother's heartbeat, the last system to suffer in the elderly is musical receptivity'. Powerful stuff.

**We hope to share with you a manual and CDs which will defuse fears about managing and using social dance.
Immerse yourself in the package and, have fun...**

THE MUSIC

Quality music, played with lift and verve, is vital to enjoyable dancing. Although many of the dances and tunes used in Britain today have their origins in the traditions of the British Isles, it is impossible to avoid being gradually influenced by the styles and practices of other countries. So we have music from France and the EU in general, from the West Indies, Jewish tunes, Bhangra from the Punjabi folk tradition, South American rhythms and so on. Callers and musicians steadily contribute new dances and new tunes to a living genre which has its roots in ancient times.

The history of the music is truly fascinating. Ivan Hewett, in his recent BBC radio programme 'In the Beginning Was the Song', provides evidence that singing and dancing are, and always have been, a key part of being human. He describes a swan bone flute dated around 33,000 BC, found in caves once inhabited by human beings in present day south-western Germany. The strong urge to sing, dance and make music - how far back does it go?

Music for church services, before the introduction of the organ, was often provided by a small band of local musicians, who would also play for social dances, sometimes held in the same building!

In the nineteenth century, in Dorset, Thomas Hardy's father and brother, and in Sussex, William Mittell from New Romney, inscribed secular tunes, new to them, along the margins and inside the back covers of their church band music books. Tunes were shared as they are now, brought by visitors, relatives and itinerant muscians. Foreign marching bands, who travelled the English countryside in summer, made a significant contribution. The German bands mentioned in *Ninfield In the Nineties*, that is the 1890s, were a typical influence. Perhaps our own military bands, returning from duties overseas, played their part in enlarging repertoires.

People such as Scan Tester (1887-1972), renowned Sussex anglo concertina player, had a wealth of tunes and a fund of stories about music and dance. He talks of elderly men step-dancing in the local: 'They'd have a step, they'd get up and cross over and make a figure of eight, several ways of doing it'.

Jim Harding, who died young in 2004, was another excellent concertina player who wrote tunes sympathetic to the tradition, notably 'Harveys' Hornpipe', named for the Lewes Brewery.

Scan, Jim and many other musicians have left a rich legacy to bands and dancers everywhere.

Itinerant musicianship dates from Medieval times and gradually music became joined with dance. Horses Branle, one of the tunes included on the accompanying CDs, dates from before 1589 when it was first published in *Orchesography*, a French dialogue document of sixteenth-century music and dance, by Thoinot Arbeau. John Aubrey, English antiquary, writing before 1697, says 'Peasants danced to the tune of the pipe and tabor in the churchyard on Holy-Day-Eves'. And the Basques still do. Later, reed, wind and stringed instruments were added, and subsequently, by the seventeenth century, brass instruments were common - to the dismay of some, who did not relish the frequent discordance and increase in decibels.

In latter years the Sussex band, The Catsfield Steamers, has come full circle, holding dances inside churches, notably with Father Christopher Hopkins at the Norman Church of St Peter and Paul, Peasmarsh, Sussex, and also at St John's Church in St Leonard's on Sea. It was once a common practice.

Father Christopher says 'Church ales, that is feastdays which included ale but also consisted of music and dancing, date back hundreds of years. Bride ales, clerk ales, lamb ales, leet ales, midsummer ales, harvest ales...'.

THE DANCE

Religious and ritual ceremonial dances were closely linked from earliest pre-Christian times. In Luxor, Egypt, rock carvings dating from 3400 BC and in Elam, modern day Iran, ceramic art shows the classic chain dance, otherwise known as a carol or circle dance. The instinct is to join hands in a circle and, perhaps, to sing whilst on the move. Today circle dances are danced in our local Unitarian Church and although regarded as a secular activity by most, some people do appreciate a spiritual element to the activity.

Early circle dances usually had a focus, a menhir or standing stone, or, as in the 1530 painting by Lucas Cranach the Elder, an apple tree.

In Helston, Cornwall, the Floral or Furry Dance is still an annual event, being a caper all around the town, and often in and out of the houses too!

There would have come a time when the purpose of religious dance blurred with the opportunity for secular dance, people having more time to enjoy activities such as seasonal fairs. We can see in Pieter Brueghel the Elder's 1560s 'The Peasant Dance' and 'The Peasant Wedding Dance', that musical instruments such as pipes and tabors, drums, and small bagpipes are being used with the dancers displaying considerable verve and energy. Brueghel the Younger's painting, 'Flemish Fair', shows the next development - a line dance, the farandole.

'Leading someone a merry dance' was originally a phrase coined from this romp from Provencal in which the dancers join hands and, amongst other moves, wind between each other in a chain known as a hey.

The linear development of courtly and country dances overlapped and progressed through the years with the French adopting our 'contre danse', sending us in return, for example, the cotillion, a four couple square dance which in turn reappears much later, from America, transformed into a brisk and bustling 'set-running' square dance.

By the eighteenth century, Assembly Rooms and the ballrooms of country houses were built in Palladian style, longer and narrower than before. This caused the development of the long set and the single couple square. Enthusiasm abounded. Some dances, for example 'The Tempest', lasted for three quarters of an hour until the exhausted fiddlers and participants all but collapsed!

Many other styles of dance were developed and enjoyed over the next two centuries but country dances were still to be found, for example, in Hindringham, Norfolk, where up until the First World War the 'frolics' were 'a bit rough and ready, but everyone enjoyed themselves, there'd be a rare old rigmarole of dancing'.

In 1889 Professor John Ruskin at Whitelands College, London, revived country dance as being suitable to be taught in schools by his teacher training college graduates, usually on wet afternoons when outdoor physical activities were limited! The English Folk Dance and Song Society, founded in 1911, enabled a further revival of interest in social dance and probably the Folk revival in the 1960s and 1970s also went a long way to re-establishing social dance in its present day popular position.

Dancing a version of the Waves of Tory (Page 41) at the Valsequillo Almond Festival in the Gran Canarian mountains was a delight. It is good to know that traditional dance is truly international.

FITTING THE DANCE TO THE MUSIC

You will notice in our 'Dance Notation' section, labelling, which may require explanation.

AABB for example would denote the four eight-bar parts of a dance which would fit its 32 - bar tune; in simple terms, count eight and eight and eight and eight to give you your 32 bars.

Both A & B parts of a tune are normally repeated as above to fulfill the requirement for four parts of a dance.

Less frequently, dances demand music of three parts or 48 bars, and such tunes are played AABBCC, CC being the third part of the tune. So here there will be six parts for the dancers to match to the music. Alternatively a 32-bar tune can be played AABBAB to achieve the same end.

Often two or more tunes are linked together to provide a lift to the dancers and extra interest to all.

Listening skills come into play when young dancers are invited to be aware of where and when the music changes.

The caller, or teacher and helpers, should 'walk' the dancers through the parts of the dance, maybe two or three times, and then, before embarking on the dance, it may be helpful to listen to a few bars of the chosen music.

The start of the dance is normally preceded by a short introduction from the band. This should give the dancers an indication of the rhythm and pace that will follow.

Having started the dance with music, the person with responsibility should 'call' the next figure at just the right place, slightly before the change of direction is needed. Call loudly and clearly, with confidence, until you recognise that dancers have become familiar with the tune and dance and no longer need your support. Be aware that sometimes some dancers will always need support! Be patient. You be the judge!

People will come to realise that in many dances their position in the set will change; they may become 'top couple', they may progress around a circle, they may change partners. Although preferable when dancers progress to new partners in a dance, there is no need to insist on different sex couples; and never pick up on someone who appears to have 'no rhythm at all'! We are aiming for a confident, beneficial enjoyment of dancing and rhythm, whatever the ability, whatever the age.

Remember, an exuberance arises from a room or hall full of willing and able dancers. People have asked us to provide music of a decent length and so, for that reason, our recorded tracks do just that. However, you can always say 'last time through' and fade out. See how your dancers feel!

WHY DANCE?

Use this pack and find out!

TYPES OF TUNES

Tunes in the British tradition are normally one of the following:

REELS are lively, in 4/4 time.

JIGS are in 6/8 time, and brisk.

POLKAS, of Bohemian, Czechoslovakian origin, although many have now been created within the British tradition, are a 1 2 3 hop circling couple dance or danced in a line with a skip to the step, in 2/4 or 4/4 time.

HORNPIPES are British tunes in 4/4 time, probably the best known example being the 'Sailor's Hornpipe'.

SCHOTTISCHES, also of Bohemian origin, use a step hop. Sometimes step left, step right, step left, and a hop step and so on for travelling a distance, or a slower paced step hop more generally used, being right hop, left hop, right hop, left hop, 2/4 time.

WALTZES in 3/4 time, a circling movement.

When calling we usually invite dancers to 'feel' the music, feel the rhythm.

Traditional music is NOT exclusively used. Use Mike Oldfield's version of 'In Dulce Jubilo' or Rednex extremely popular 'Cotton Eye Joe'. Try Gary Glitter's 'Another Rock and Roll Christmas' with King Offa's Delight, page 32, a lovely partner matched hop step, great fun!

Children and adults alike will have fun setting known and invented dances to their own contemporary musical favourites.

You will find our chosen music has been associated in the pack with dances at several differentiated levels. This means the WHY DANCE? pack may be used, as our title page describes, with a lunchtime or after school club, with youth clubs, guide, scout, cub or brownie packs, with family groups as a fundraiser in schools, for a complete dance with adults...

**GENTLEMEN ALWAYS HAVE THEIR LADY ON THEIR RIGHT,
UNLESS ADVISED OTHERWISE.**

EXPLANATIONS FOR TECHNICAL WORDS PRINTED IN **BOLD** WILL BE FOUND IN THE GLOSSARY; READ IT FIRST!

THE SET OF DANCES PRESCRIBED FOR EACH TUNE INCREASE IN DIFFICULTY.

DANCE WITH CHILDREN, AND THE CURRICULUM

Dance in schools now involves statutory curricular criteria and that includes traditional dance. However it is used, enjoyment should remain at the heart. Teachers, and perhaps, in extra-curricular clubs, classroom assistants, mid-day supervisory assistants and even parents have an opportunity to join in with pupil partners. This itself becomes a successful strategy where, at times, no-one in the room feels especially confident!

These challenges can help to develop the skills, concepts and ideas behind the genre. We know that if social dance is experienced from early years without fear of coercion or ridicule, and celebrated for its vigour, stamina and the pleasure it imparts, it can become a powerful tool, influencing behaviour beyond school walls. More experienced children may act as support assistants to younger classes, or in clubs, demonstrating and developing dance. All types of dance are currently experiencing a renaissance, children's imaginations have been caught, and traditional, heritage dance merits its place.

> In 2008 Andy Burnham, Secretary of State at the Department for Culture, Media and Sport, (www.culture.gov.uk) said 'It is time for the government to be positive in its response to the impact that dance is having amongst young people by giving them proper support.... for the first time dance will have a national youth strategy run by Dance Youth England'. Those of us who are passionate about traditional dance must ensure it keeps its place amongst other styles in the genre.

Such dancing can:

- be an exploration of wonderful music with its upbeat rhythmic patterns and phrasing.
- aid children's physical control, fluency and co-ordination of movement, treading a fine line between individual freedom and the constraints of team structure.
- build a set of experiences which may be celebrated, honed and displayed.
- be an excellent activity for both mental and physical health and well being.

Thus we can see that social dance provides some answers to three of the four core themes of the current National Healthy Schools Programme:

- Physical activity.
- Emotional health and well being.
- Personal, social and health education.

> **Government reports give frightening figures for obesity levels and mental health problems amongst even the youngest children. Dance can be one physical activity which balances energy intake and expenditure levels, thus reducing storage of body fat. Regular exercise is known to alleviate stress and anxiety and, furthermore, social dance can develop positive attitudes to other physical activities. Even some reluctant boys become interested when they understand the stamina and strength levels involved in some of the dances.**

The use of traditional, social dance in schools can be further encouraged when looked at beside the statutory strands of learning for physical education set out in the government web site, www.curriculumonline.qca.org.uk, where curriculum areas require four key points, namely that:

- Children acquire and develop new skills.

- Children select and apply learnt skills.
- Children have a knowledge and understanding of fitness and health.
- Evaluation and aims towards improvement be an essential part of children's activities.

P.E. (NC) KS1 and 2; create and perform dances using a range of movement patterns (simple patterns at KS1) including those from different times and cultures.
See www.standards.dfes.gov.uk for specifics.

Dances can, of course also be adapted to suit demands; not only can there be cross-curricular application within teaching frameworks but also sheer enjoyment! Scatter Polka can be danced like a game - see how many different people you can dance with. King Offa's Delight can have substituted moves called by a chosen caller, sit down, stand up, jump in the air, turn round etc. The Pawn Broker and Spitfire tell stories of their own (see Dance Notation) and King Offa's Delight has had movements substituted which represent the story of a Harvest, the dance being performed at half speed for special needs children.

The original Christmas 'carol' was a circle dance, thus it would be appropriate for shepherds to dance a celebration of Christ's birth. Applying traditional dance to alternative Christmas music, to sung carols or to secular music would be an enjoyable diversion. Dances can also be deliberately created to fit specific occasions; a centenary event produced a circle dance representing the cake, with an inner circle of dancers, arms raised in arches, being candles. Thus Personal, Social and Health Education, History and Religious Education may be addressed. And, if there was to be a cross curricular approach through 'six themed areas of learning', then heritage dance could certainly be a valid component.

We have found that children as young as four and a half, ie those in Early Years schooling, respond enthusiastically to elements of traditional dance. Many cannot yet skip, they cannot turn under another's arm but, as their spatial awareness and muscle control develops, they can, even at this early age, begin to be part of a group moving to music. Dances must obviously be simple and consist of only a few remembered elements but they soon learn left from right and they very quickly express and ask for their favourite dances.

Some points worth remembering;

- Country dancing can be very energetic; inhalers at the ready.
- Use hair ruffles/bands on the right wrist as a mnemonic.
- Let couples pick each other; do not insist on opposite sexes.
- In Strip the Willow, the 'men' wearing wristbands or a coloured PE band will help dancers spot their next partner.
- Walk through dances enough times to help children appreciate that they will probably change positions, and maybe partners, several times during the dance. Age and ability will dictate the need. Ask them to anticipate their final destination!
- Continue to call, even if it appears children are remembering the moves; help them to consolidate the activity in their minds.

Excellence and enjoyment, that is the core, and we believe that this book and CDs provide opportunities for both.

DANCE WITH ADULTS

Folk Dance or Traditional Dance clubs local to your area can easily be found on the Web and at your local library. These clubs usually meet weekly and sometimes for special Saturday night ceilidhs (dances), with a song or two perhaps, or for events such as New Year's Eve. Try one out, see if the music is really varied and conducive to dancing! At these events a variety of callers and leaders take it in turns to run evenings and instruct participants in the chosen set of dances. There are often opportunities for people to try calling a dance for themselves. New music of a suitable length for all dancers to have their turn is always welcome. Introduce this pack's CDs!

We find that an adaption of dances for older folk is much appreciated, those who no longer enjoy too much spinning or jumping, for whom a promenade down the set is safer than sidestepping down and for whom 'down and back' need be only half way and not all the way.

Folk or traditional music festivals are excellent events for young people to discover that traditional dance can have a zest and an energy that appeals to them, where boys and girls, young men and women especially, can find a response to the often demanding movements, and the huge variety of exciting music on offer. Festivals can provide cheap, revitalising holidays with plenty of dances: Sidmouth, Cambridge, Whitby, Broadstairs, Chester, Towersey, Cheltenham, Bromsgrove (www.folkandroots.co.uk or www.efdss.org). Learn some dances from these CDs and book, and go and have some fun!

Why not seek out or start a Family Barn Dance Club? Children from age six or seven enjoy dancing in the company of adults, often their memories and responses are better, they dance wholeheartedly, as we have seen at wedding dances, which *have* to be amongst the most sociable of all occasions. With a considerate caller it is possible to have people from 'nine to ninety' up dancing, so long as someone is responsible for keeping the babies out of harms way!

ഈ൦ര

PUTTING ON A DANCE

Whoever is doing the planning, a dance may be purely a social community event, celebratory, or more regular, or specifically a fundraiser. A small group of friends is best for sharing the organisational load, some people with a committed interest in spreading the word too, to boost ticket sales!

Youth organisations very often set challenges for their members, for example, at the moment, Girlguiding UK have a project, **'Go for it!'** which gives participants the opportunity to plan, undertake and produce an event, which could be a dance. This may eventually spread beyond the guide group and their friends, community action being one of their core values.

So you have a purpose!

Church, village or school halls make excellent venues as they have the required toilets, kitchens, waste disposal and often a stage where the caller may see and be seen. Halls differ tremendously in cost and quality, they have participant number limits and the closer they are to residential buildings the earlier you will be required to end your evening. Check that the floor is dancer friendly, but otherwise even the grimmest looking venue can be camouflaged inside with greenery and paper table coverings, tea lights and hung streamers, to create a suitable atmosphere.

Barns, although cheap, large and offering useful parking areas, are probably best avoided, especially compacted dung floors which, along with hay and straw bales, can quickly exacerbate asthma and other lung complaints in the dancers as they, literally, 'kick up the dust'. They can be cold even in summer. Cement floor barns, well swept of dust, are a possibility and will be very picturesque hung with garlands of greenery. Again watch for uneven or slippery dance areas and protruding farm machinery and encourage people to cover bales which they are using as seating.

For very special events there may be marquees, but now we are raising the costs!

So you have a venue!

Your chairs and tables should be placed along the walls as close to the focus, that is caller and music, as possible, not in a group at the other end of the room! If there is no stage the caller should work on a short wall end of the room giving a long view down, otherwise she/he will quickly develop a stiff neck! In long sets the dancers stand with their side to the caller, facing their partners and the men having their backs to the caller's right hand wall, ladies facing them.

Do keep a watchful eye on dancers, young and old; their happiness, comfort and enjoyment are the caller's main responsibility. Dances can go completely wrong, but they can always be restarted. Care of the audience is a caller's vital role.

A drinks bar should be part of the same room and certainly not elsewhere in the venue, thus ensuring that you keep your dancers together; some newcomers may be a little uncertain and reluctant at first. Remember there are legal criteria for getting, stocking and staffing an outside bar with alcoholic drinks; it is sometimes easier for people to bring their own drinks, and a supper too. Perhaps you could invite a fish'n'chip van or other outside caterers assured of a good customer base, to call at an appointed time.

So you can create a convivial atmosphere!

Consider this; can you reconcile a suitable ticket price, enough ticket sales, and the cost of the hall and decorations? Advertising with the help of computer-produced fliers can be of minimal expense - be creative in finding legal places to leave them. If you are fundraising, remember that a raffle with some reasonable prizes can probably raise a pound per dancer attending, especially if you have enthusiastic, persuasive sellers. Do be confident on these points.

So you have a budget!

The caller should plan and consider a set of dances with varied music, and a mixture of rhythms. Call easier dances and, more importantly, dances with which you feel most confident, early in the evening. There can be inexpensive spot prizes - all ages enjoy this, especially if you sometimes invent spurious reasons for them! Dance for about ninety or so minutes but be flexible. Consider ages, the weather - several other factors may crop up which mean more, or less dancing before stopping for a break. Consider the evening's finishing time, allowing time for clearing up - work backwards, timing your second session to begin after some supper and that raffle.

And remember, you have our permission to use the two CDs in this pack in Public Performance.

You have the makings of an excellent evening!

BIBLIOGRAPHY

Thoinot Arbeau, *Orchesography: a treatise in the form of a dialogue, whereby all manner of persons may easily acquire and practice the honourable exercise of dancing* (1588; translated by Mary Stewart Evans, New York: Dover Publications, 1967)

Les Barclay and Ian Jones, editors, *Community Dance Manual* (London: English Folk Dance and Song Society [EFDSS], Revised complete edition, 2005)

Sibyl Clark, *English Folk Dancing for Schools and Junior Youth Clubs* (London: EFDSS, 1975, ISBN 085418094X)

Sibyl Clark and Mary Evans, *Swing Partners: an introduction to English Social Dancing* (London: Novello for EFDSS, 1964)

Jimmy Clossin and Carl Hertzog, *The American Cowboy Square Dance Book* (London: Bell, 1952)

Ann-Marie Hulme and Peter Clifton, 'Social Dancing in a Norfolk Village 1900-1945', *Folk Music Journal*, vol. 3, no. 4 (1978) pp 359-370

Priscilla and Robert Lobley, *Your Book of English Country Dancing* (London: Faber & Faber, 1980, ISBN 0571115225)

Belinda Quirey, *May I have the Pleasure? The Story of Popular Dancing* (London: BBC, 1976, ISBN 056311007; 2nd ed. London: Dance, 1987, ISBN 1852730005)

Alfred T Ridel, *Ninfield in the Nineties: reminiscences of village life in all its activities.* (Ninfield: Privately published, [1979])

Hugh Rippon, *Discovering English Folk Dance* (Princes Risborough: Shire Publications, 3rd ed. 1993, ISBN 0747802254)

Christopher Weir, *Village and Town Bands* (Aylesbury: Shire Publications, 1981, ISBN 085263519)

www.curriculumonline.qca.org.uk

www.girlguiding.org.uk

www.wellcometrust.ac.uk

TRACK and TUNE LIST

We thought it appropriate to record music of a length that will enable each dancer in a set to complete the notated dance at least once through the figures before the music stops. We hope that this approach will provide a practical resource to users such as dance clubs, who may wish to fit their own dances to the tunes.

As with our dances, every effort has been made to research and credit the provenance of each piece, but, when a tune has been passed from musician to musician by ear, it is sometimes difficult to pinpoint both where it was first heard and its origins. We would be grateful for any information providing greater detail on the origins of any piece of music listed here and recorded on the accompanying CDs.

Take some time to listen and practise spotting the musical introductions. These cue you to where the dancing actually begins.

Compact Disc One

Track 1: Whitehaven Volunteers / Harvey's Hornpipe* (English Polkas)

Track 2: Lillibulero / Picking of Sticks (Irish Jigs)

Track 3: La Fleur de Bruyer (French Jig)

Track 4: Mona's Delight / Scholar's Reel (Schottisches)

Track 5: Polkas de l'Avayron (French Polkas)

Track 6: The New Rigged Ship / The Duke of Atholl's Reel (Scottish Jigs)

Track 7: Fanny Power / Planxty Irwin (Irish Waltzes)

Track 8: The Kite** / The Jewish Tune

Compact Disc Two

Track 1: The Braes of Tollymet / Harry Cox's Schottische (Schottisches)

Track 2: La Ronde de la Millereine (French Jig) / Title unknown

Track 3: News of the Victory / Woodland Flowers (English Jigs)

Track 4: The Horses Brawl (French Branle).

Track 5: The New Victory / Down The Road (English Polkas)

Track 6: The Sweets Of May / Dingles Regatta (Irish Jigs)

Track 7: Terribus / The 42nd Highlanders' Farewell to Gibraltar (Scottish Marches)

Bonus Track **Track 8:** Worcestershire Hornpipe (English)

All tunes traditional, arranged The Catsfield Steamers except those marked *

*1/1(b) Written by Jim Harding of Eastbourne

**1/8(a) Written by Keith Leech of Hastings

The CDs accompanying this book may be used in public performance.

CD 1/1: - Whitehaven Volunteers / Harveys' Hornpipe ~ 32 bar polkas

Flying Scotsman

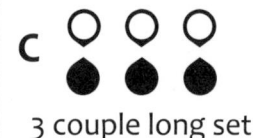

A1   Ladies hold hands along their line. **Top lady** leads all the others around behind her partner, and weaves between her partner and the next man, in front of him, behind the third and back to place.

A2   Gentlemen do the same, top man leads the gentlemen to weave in the same way.

B1 & 2   **Top couple** only, hold both hands, take four small side steps down the middle of the set and back to place. Top couple go down the set again and as they get to the end of the set everyone else hold hands with their partner, following the top couple down the room for four more side steps. All return, swinging partner round, ready to start the dance again, with a new top couple, the original top couple now being at the bottom of the set; everyone else has moved up one place. **Progression.**

Jargon Buster: Progression, one of many ways in which dancers will meet new couples.

If using this dance with young children why not add a few train noises as the lines lead round! A less tiring version of A1 would be for the middle man to step back enabling the ladies to more easily achieve their goal.

3 couple long set

The Tempest

A1   All eight people join hands, circle left back to place with a **rant** step.

A2   Everyone take their partner in a two hand or **ballroom hold** and rant eight steps across the set, ie those facing the caller move towards him/her and those with their backs to the caller move away from him/her. Return to place.

B1   The four people in the middle of the set make a right and left hand **star** while the end gentlemen **swing** the lady who is facing them.

B2   Back in original places, join hands along the line of four, rant four steps forward, and back to place, clap own hands together 3 times. Those with their backs to the caller join hands and make **arches** and those facing them go underneath. DO NOT turn round; there will be another line of dancers to greet you, ready to start again.

BUT lines reaching either end of the room will find that they have no one to dance with; they turn round to face the other dancers, gentlemen swapping sides with their ladies so that their partner is again on their right hand side, they stand out of the next round of the dance, but get ready for the following one when there will be another line of four dancers to greet them.

Jargon Buster: Rant, see glossary. If your dancers are disinclined to rant, a **polka** step is more than adequate.

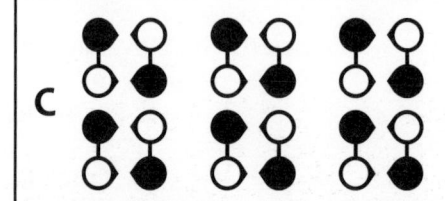

Double Sicilian, in a straight set. Danced traditionally, but not necessarily, to a **rant** step.

Kerry Polka

64 bars: Twice the given music = Once through the dance.

Couples numbered 1, 2, 3, 4. See Glossary **Square Set**.

A1 & 2   In a **ballroom hold** and staying on the spot, couples 'dip' their joined hands downward into the square and back. Couples dance a turning **polka** so that everyone moves one place anticlockwise. Repeat three more times until back in original places.

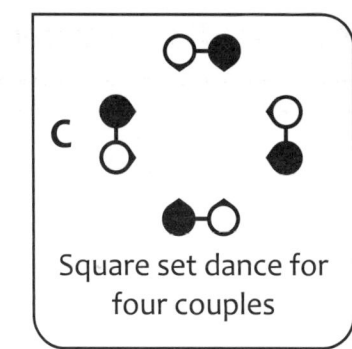

B1   Ladies right hand **star** half way round the set to the opposite man, **setting** right and left once, and dance each other round on the spot.

B2   Men left hand star half way round back to their original partners, setting right and left once, and dance each other round on the spot.

C1   1s and 3s hold inside hands with their partner, dance forward towards each other and back twice. Ballroom hold and polka across the set, turning as you dance, ending up in your original spot.

C2   2s and 4s hold inside hands with their partner, dance forward towards each other and back twice. Ballroom hold and polka across the set, turning as you dance, ending up in your original spot.

D1 & 2   **Grand chain**, back to places and dance your partner if there is music left.

Pick up your feet when you pick up the rhythm!

Square set dance for four couples

Throughout this manual

● Represents the Gentleman   ○ Represents the Lady

The caller (C) is on the left hand side of all the accompanying diagrams.

Gentlemen always have their lady on their right, unless advised otherwise.

Please make your own nomenclature choices regarding
Ladies / Gentleman / Gents - Men / Women - Boys / Girls

Explanations for technical words printed in bold
will be found in the glossary.

The set of dances prescribed for each tune increases in difficulty and remember these tunes are not exclusive to these dances. Swap jigs, for example, with other jigs from the list that better suit your purpose.

CD 1/2: - Lillibulero / Picking of Sticks ~ 32 bar jigs

Circassian Circle

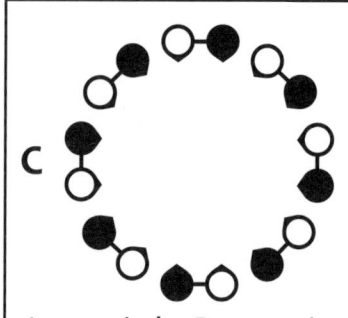

A1   All join hands, four steps in and back out again.

       Repeat.

A2   All the ladies three steps in and instead of the fourth step, jump in the air, clap their hands, and back out again.

       Repeat, men doing the same.

B1   **Swing** partner.

B2   **Promenade** partner around the room in anticlockwise direction, ladies leave their partner and move on to the next gentleman. All join hands to start again!

Large circle. Progressive if required. Very often used as final dance.

If dancing this with young children or wanting to encourage everyone to join in, irrespective of whether they have a partner or not, the progression can be left out. B1 & B2 can be replaced by circling left and right and everyone stays with their own partner or partners.

A2 As people jump you may like to encourage them to 'Yeehah!' Younger children love to shout the name of their school etc.

Oxo Reel

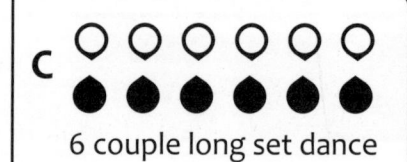

A1   All join hands along the lines (ie all ladies' line hold hands, and all men's line hold hands).

       Lines go forward four steps to meet each other and back to place. **Do si do** your partner.

A2   Repeat.

B1   Oxo! Top two couples join hands to make a circle. Bottom two couples do the same, they circle left and right, at the same time the middle two couples right hand **star** then left hand star.

B2   Top couple **swing** partner round, at the same time making their way down to the bottom of the set. Everyone else clap and cheer them!

6 couple long set dance

Variation:

A1   Lines forward and back, top couple galop to the bottom of the set.

A2   Lines forward and back, the next top couple galop to end of set.

B1   Oxo as above.

B2   Bottom couple swing back up to the top.

Dashing White Sergeant

A1 All six people join hands, circle left, then back to the right returning to place.

A2 Gentleman turns to face the lady on his right and they **set** to each other, and the same to his other lady.

B1 He right arm turns this lady, then a left arm turn with the one on his left. Repeat this move.

B2 Trios join hands along their line and dance forward four steps, and back to place. Moving forward, travel out to the right, pass the trio they have just danced with and slot back into place facing a new trio.

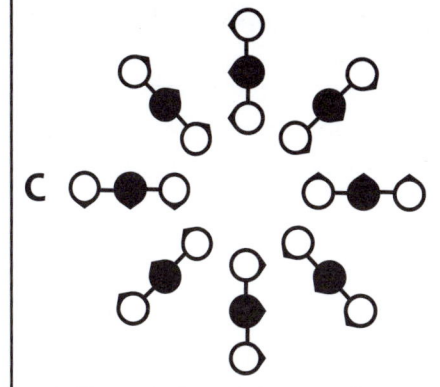

Sicilian circle made up of trios, a gentleman between two ladies, facing each other all the way around the room

Jargon Buster: Setting, a couple, facing each other, step simultaneously to the right and back to the left twice, lightly on the ball of the foot.

Callers should encourage the trios to look ahead to spot their new opposites!

Dave Robert's Dingle aka Pride of Pingle

Ken Alexander

A1 Turning their backs on the caller and holding up their joined inside hands, the four couples dance down the room, with the Dingle dancing up underneath their arches. All turn and back to places.

Four couple long set, with a fifth member, the Dingle, facing the caller, between the fourth couple. Progressive.

A2 *Information! The Dingle has to reach the top of the set by joining in with each couple's right and left hand turn.*

Everyone right hand turn their partner with the Dingle joining the bottom couple, almost immediately she/he will face the next couple up ready to join in with their left hand turn. The Dingle will pass on the next couple up with their right hand and a left to the top couple.

B1 Join hands down each row with the Dingle bustling in to join on the top of the appropriate side. Lines forward and back twice, during which the Dingle's line is jostled down so that everyone has a new partner and a new Dingle is dropped off at the end.

B2 **Swing** your new partner, turn your backs on caller to start again.

A2 *If using this dance with young and/or inexperienced people the Dingle can run round each couple as they right and left hand turn - 'chasing the snake' to the top of the set.*

Boston Tea Party

A1 Top couple holding inside hands dance to the bottom of the set. Still keeping hold, the lady dances in front of her partner to the outside of the gentlemen's row and that couple take a single **arch** over the gentlemen to the top.

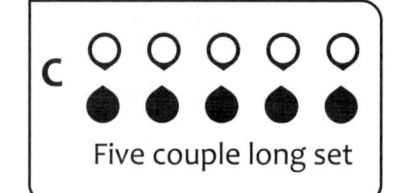

A2 Top couple repeat the procedure with the gentlemen moving out and they bring an arch back up over the ladies row.

B1 Top couple **Dip and Dive**. At the same time, as the tops pass, each couple **casts** out to the bottom of the set, under the arch and back up the set.

B2 **Swing** partners.

Five couple long set

Nervous Breakdown — David Mills

A1 Everyone turn and face their partner, **NB travelling will all be done in this direction,** right hand turn, back to your place, then let go and move on one place, past your partner in the direction you are facing.

Facing this new partner, left arm turn and move on.

A2 Two handed turn with this person, and again move on.

Do si do this one but DO NOT MOVE ON.

B1 Take this new partner by both hands and **balance** twice, and turn your partner round once.

B2 All join hands back in a large circle, gentlemen making sure they have their lady on their right. Four steps in, out and repeat again. Turn and face your partner ready to start all over again.

As the name implies, this dance is hectic and children love it!

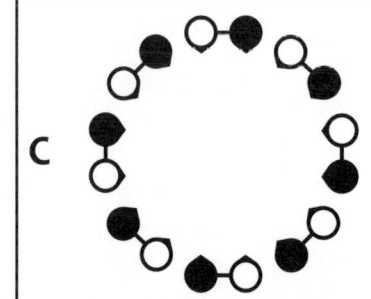

Large circle for as many couples as will. Progressive.

For your own notes

CD 1/3:- La Fleur de Bruyer ~ 48 bar jig

Florida Snowball Martin Hodges

Couples number themselves up 1, 2, 3, 4, 5 from the top of the set.

- A1 First couple right arm turn, then left arm turn.
- A2 1s and 2s, right hand **star**, then left hand star.
- B1 1s, 2s and 3s join hands, circle left and right.
- B2 1s, 2s, 3s and 4s join hands in a circle, take four steps in and out, and repeat.
- C1 & 2 Fifth couple galop up the set and return to the bottom **cast**ing out with everyone following. This couple make an arch at the top end of set and everyone goes underneath, swiftly.

  5s should now be at the top of the set ready to right arm turn, everyone else has moved down one place.

Five couple long set

Drops of Brandy

This dance is usually un-phrased, so you do not need A1, A2 etc, as the dancers will progress at their own pace.

Top couple half **Strip the Willow**, down the set, the lady going out to the men's side with the man waiting for her in the middle each time, then work back up again with the man going out to the ladies' side and his lady waiting in the middle.

Long set for as many as will or the number of couples that would suit your choice of variation

When back at the top of the set, that same couple do a full Strip the Willow to the bottom.

Now the dance starts all over again with the next top couple; they need not wait for the previous dancers to reach the bottom of the set.

Variation:

Long set for as many as will for a continuous Strip the Willow!

Top couple Strip the Willow to the bottom of the set; after they have moved down a couple of places the next couple join in.   A Mexican Wave Strip the Willow maybe!

Willow Tree   Hugh Ripon

Eight couple long set

A1   Top couple galop down the set, the gentleman leaves his lady behind and brings the bottom lady back up the set.

A2   Bottom man brings the lady back up to the top and takes his own partner back down to their place.

B1 & 2   Top and bottom couple both **Strip the Willow**, three times, the top couple moving down the set and the bottom couple moving up the set to meet in the middle. These couples join hands to make a circle, and raising their arms, make four arches, the 'Willow Tree'.

C1 & 2   At this point it's best to describe the set as two separate halves joined in the middle by the 'Willow Tree'. Those at the top half of the set, face up, those at the bottom face down, the leader of each row **casts** out, away from their partner and down the outside and under the side of the 'Willow Tree'. Here you will find your partner to dance back to your own original end of the set and swing.

This dance won't go wrong if you remember that the top half of the set NEVER dance/change places with the bottom half during the last two moves. HOWEVER, an experienced set could have a 'Willow Tree' which circles left, simply to swap halves before the casting dancers arrive at their arches. This will produce a lot of fun!

Square Strip the Willow

Square set dance for four couples

Couples with their backs to the caller and facing the caller are head couples, the other two couples at the side of the set are side couples.

A1   Head couples, holding both hands with their partner, galop eight steps across the set, and back.

A2   Side couples the same.

B1 & 2   *Explanation! The head men are going to **Strip the Willow** round the set with each lady in turn, travelling to their right until they return to their own partner. Invite these two men to consider and remember each lady in turn; his right hand lady, his opposite lady, his left hand lady and his own. Second time round the side men Strip the Willow, third time, the head ladies and fourth time the side ladies. Obviously the ladies are considering each man in turn. Encourage the people who are waiting to be danced with to offer their left hand. This is especially useful when you have same sex groups.*

Head men 'Strip the Willow', give each other their right arm turning three quarters round and giving their left arm to that right hand lady, turn her once and right arm back to the man in the middle, left turn the opposite lady, right arm the man in the middle, left turn the next lady, right arm the man in the middle, left turn their partner.

C1   All join hands, circle eight left and right.

C2   Polka your partner around the set back to place, turning around as you dance.

Jargon Buster: Polka, 123 hop circling couple dance.

> **CD 1/4: - Mona's Delight / Scholar's Reel** ~ 32 bar schottisches, a 'syncopated' rhythm. **Step hop.** *Or use* **CD 2/8**

Clopton Bridge   John Chapman

Four couple long set

A1   Top lady and bottom man right arm turn, then left arm turn, using up all the music.

A2   Top man and bottom lady do the same.

B1   Two middle couples (who have not danced yet), right hand **star** and then, unusually, turn away left, right round to form a left hand star and dance back to place.

B2   Top couple take a two handed or **ballroom hold** and **swing** their partner down to the bottom of the set; as they pass by, everyone swing. Alternatively top couple start swinging during B1, or top couple **promenade** down the set in stately fashion and everybody swing.

Monastery aka Circle Hornpipe

16 bars: Twice through the dance = Once through the music

*Note. We always use the **ballroom hold** in this dance even with children; they enjoy trying it out!*

This has a lovely syncopated rhythm that we're sure everyone will slot into after a couple of rounds.

Double circle, ladies on the inside facing out towards their partner. Progressive.

A1   Four side steps, with attitude, to the gentleman's left and four back again. Two steps to the gentleman's left and two back again. Everyone claps their own hands together, clap right hand on your partner's right, your own hands together, left hand with partner's left, clap own hands together, cross hands across chest and clap both hands on to partner's; the music at this point allows you to say 'POOM'.

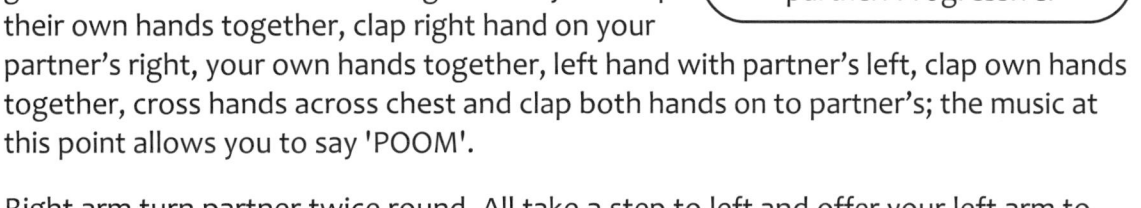

A2   Right arm turn partner twice round. All take a step to left and offer your left arm to the next person along, for a left arm turn. Keep this new partner, ballroom hold, ready to start again.

Mon Reve Schottische   as seen in the film 'Chocolat'

A couple dance; place yourselves anywhere in the room, with a **ballroom hold**; a laid-back **step hop** rhythm.

Two steps to the man's left, two steps back again and dance your partner round for four steps.

Malthouse

16 bars: Twice through the dance = Once through the music

Hold right hands with partner and left hand to person next door. DO NOT CROSS HANDS. This will leave you with a space in front of you, into which you can move.

Double circle, men on the inside facing out. Progressive.

A1   Two **step hops** into the space you have in front of you, two steps back out, let go to hold both hands with your partner, dance four small step hops round, so that the men end up on the outside.
Right hand to your partner, left to one next door again. Dance two steps into the space in front of you, and back out again. Hold both hands with your partner and dance four small hop steps round so that the men are back on the inside, still holding hands.

A2   Men 'push' their lady four step hops out of the circle, using all the music, and 'pull' her four steps back into the middle.
Everyone take a step left to their new partner and left arm turn them round once, ready to start again.

For your own notes

CD 1/5: - Polkas de l'Avayron ~ 32 bar polkas
These tunes usefully increase in speed.

Pat-a-Cake Polka

16 bars: Twice through the dance = Once through the music

Dancers take their partner anywhere on to the floor, facing the caller, avoiding standing in rows and gentlemen with their partners in a two handed or **ballroom hold**.

A1   Couples start the dance with the foot nearest the caller. Put your heel down, bring that toe to your other foot, heel and toe again and galop four side steps up the room towards the caller.

Repeat the heel and toe twice, facing and galoping in the opposite direction.

A2   Face your partner for some clapping; right hands x 3, left hands x 3, your knees x 3, your own hands x 3, then maybe **swing** partner. A variation may be to clap your hands behind your partners back and go into a swing.

Repeat, to complete the tune.

Muffin Man

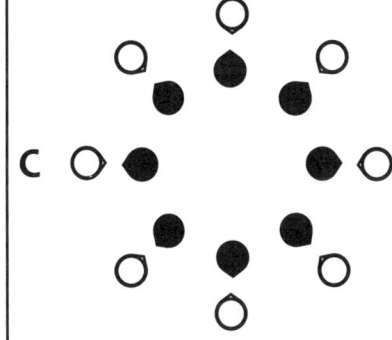

A1   Take partner in **ballroom hold** or two handed hold and galop eight side steps to the men's left and eight steps back again.

A2   Let go, and make two circles, holding hands next door. All side step eight to the left, circles going in opposite directions, and back again to face partner.

B1   Clap your own hands together and under right leg, own hands together, under left leg, together, behind you and three times quite quickly on your partner's hands.

Double circle. Men on the inside facing their partner on the outside. Progressive (if required).

Repeat clapping sequence.

B2   Everyone take a step to the left and **swing** new partners. Prepare to ballroom hold and start again.

When dancing with young children or a group who do not want to progress, change B2 to swing your partner or your choice of variation.

Cumberland Square Eight

64 bars: Once through the dance = Twice through the music

Couples with their backs to the caller and facing the caller are head couples, the other two couples at the side of the set are side couples.

Square set dance for four couples

A1 & 2   Head couples take their partner in two handed or **ballroom hold** and galop eight steps across the set and beyond, then back again to place.

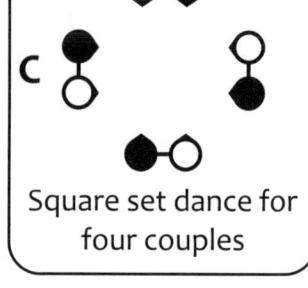

   Side couples do the same.

B1 & 2   Head couples right hand **star** and then a left hand star.

   Side couples do the same.

C1 & 2   Head couples **basket.**

   Side couples do the same.

D1 & 2   All four couples join hands and circle left for the whole eight bars, then **promenade** their partners back in the opposite direction, to places, ready to start again.

When dancing this with children substitute the basket with circle left, or use your or their imaginations.

For your own notes

CD 1/6: - The New Rigged Ship (Jig) / The Duke of Atholl's Reel ~ 32 bar

Dance to Amelia's Birthday

- A1   Everyone right arm turn, then left arm turn their partner.
- A2   Two handed turn, then **do si do** their partner.
- B1   Top couple galop down the set eight steps and back.
- B2   **Cast and arch**.

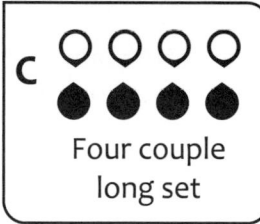

Four couple long set

Lucky Seven

- A1   Everyone join hands and circle left.
- A2   Everyone four steps into the middle and back again x 2.
- B1   Partners face each other and start off a **Grand Chain**, counting as they pass each person. Counting their partner as No 1, stop at the seventh.
- B2   **Swing** the seventh. Join hands ready to start again.

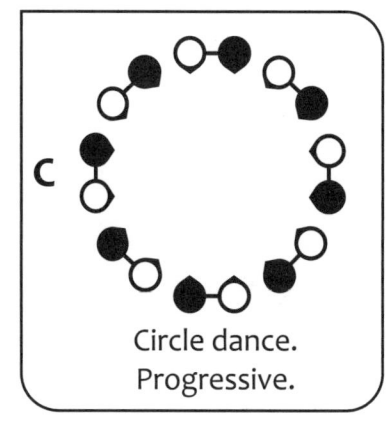

Variation:

A1 & 2   Circle left and into the middle and out a few steps, circle right and in and out again.

If dancing with children, treat this as a game; if after seven someone hasn't got a partner, they are out and go into the middle of the circle. How many are still left dancing at the end? Enterprising dancers will quickly find themselves new partners!

Circle dance. Progressive.

Circle Grab

- A1   Galop eight steps to the man's left, grab the next person to the left of your partner and galop back with them.
- A2   Grab next person to left of your partner, galop eight to the man's left again, grab the next to your left and galop eight back, KEEP THIS ONE.
- B1   Clap, on your knees x 2, right hands with partner x 2, right arm turn.
  Clap knees x 2, left hands with partner x 2, left arm turn.
- B2   **Swing** your partner.

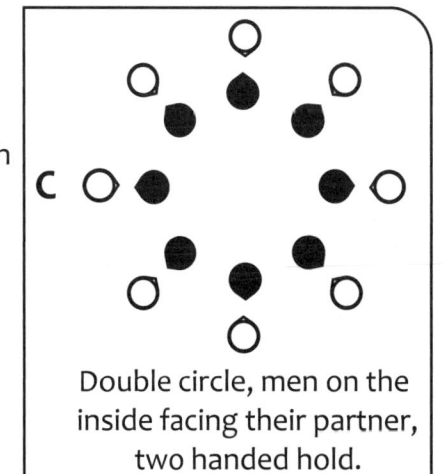

Double circle, men on the inside facing their partner, two handed hold. Progressive.

Country Bumpkin Michael Barraclough

Couples number themselves 1, 2, 3, 4, 5 from the top of the set.

Five couple long set

A1 No 1 lady and No 2 man, and No 4 lady and No 5 man right arm turn, then left.

A2 No 2 lady and No 1 man, and No 5 lady and No 4 man, right arm turn, then left.

B1 & 2 Everyone face up the set (towards the caller) and the top couple face each other. The top couple give each other their right hands and start a **Grand Chain** so that the men and the women change sides followed by the others in their line, until the top couple reach each other at the bottom of the set. They make an arch and as everyone runs out of anyone to make a chain with they continue down the outside and under the arch. **Swing** partners round to end up back on their correct side.

A simplified variation on this dance is:

A1 *Right arm turn your partner and then left arm turn.*

A2 *Everyone hold hands along their line. Take four steps forward and back again to place. The men raise their arms to make arches and the two sides swap over, and stay there.*

B1 & 2 *Complete the dance as above, dancers will return to their original sides at the end of the swing.*

We also like:

A1 *Everyone join hands along their line, take four steps forward, back and swap sides.*

A2 *Top couple galop to the end of the set and back and complete the dance as above.*

Maggy's Square Set

Couples numbered 1, 2, 3, 4. See Glossary **Square Set**.

Square set dance for four couples

A1 No 1 couple go through the middle of the set in between the No 3s, turn away from each other and weave through the dancers on the side of the set, back to place.

A2 Men make a left hand **star** and as they get to the lady on the opposite side of the set they collect her by linking arms or putting an arm round her waist. Continue all the way round, dropping her off in her place and continuing round back to their partner, offering a right hand ready to **Grand Chain**.

B1 & 2 Grand Chain back to place and a quick **swing**.

The dance starts off again with the No 2 couple going across the middle of the set in between the No 4s, casting out and weaving back round the sides of the set to place. The third time through, the No 3s start the dance off etc.

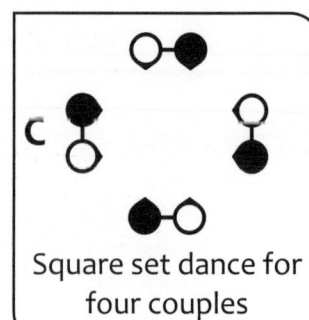

CD 1/7: Fanny Power / Planxty Irwin ~ 32 bar waltzes

Circle Waltz

16 bars: Twice through the dance = Once through the music

A1 All join hands, sway a step into the circle and out. Gentlemen pass the lady from their left hand side putting her onto their right. Repeat this three more times.

A2 Gentlemen take both hands with their partner (on his right), **chassee** two steps into the middle, and out again, take a step closer to each other, step apart and swap sides, the lady turning under the man's right arm; some call this a jive turn. Repeat this turn again.
Take partner into a ballroom hold and **waltz** around following the circle.

Note – In A1 to prevent giddiness, ladies may prefer a straight line move right rather than a turn.

Large circle, gentlemen with their lady on the right hand side. Progressive.

Chip's Waltz   Brian Scowcroft, arranged by Jane Downes

16 bars: Twice through the dance = Once through the music

A1 Taking your partner in a ballroom hold, chassee four steps to the man's left, keeping their joined hands together, couples let go their other hands turning to face the way they have come, trailing their loose hands out. Turn towards each other, bringing those loose hands together, letting go the other hand and sway out in the opposite direction and back into the ballroom hold.
Chassee four steps to the right and this time letting go joined hands, couples turn out, trailing free hands, turn towards each other, bringing those joined hands together again, letting go their other hands and sway out in the opposite direction.

A2 Join both hands with your partner and step closer together, step further apart and the gentleman twirls the lady under his right arm so that she ends up on the inside of the circle. Repeat this movement back to original places. Everybody looks and moves to the left and takes a ballroom hold with the next person on the left and waltzes anticlockwise with them in the circle. Get ready to start the moves again with this new partner.

Double circle, men on the inside. Ballroom hold.

The Rozsa Waltz Gordon Potts

16 bars: Twice through the dance = Once through the music

Couples take their partner anywhere on to the floor, gentlemen with their backs to the middle of the room.

A1   Facing his partner the gentleman holds his hands up in front of him (about chest height) and his lady places her palms onto his. The gentleman now sways his hands to the right, left and back to the right again, then lifting his lady's left hand with his right, she turns to her right, ducking her head, and turning away from him, she now has her back to her partner, with his arms round her, do not let go! Together they take four small side steps to their right.
Still in this hold, the couple take four steps to their left, sway right, sway left, sway right and uncurl so that they are facing each other again.

A2   Gentleman takes his partner's right hand into his right hand, they take a step closer towards each other, step apart, and swap sides, the lady turning under the man's right arm; some call this a jive turn. Repeat this again.
Take partner in **ballroom hold** and **waltz** around.

The hold and turn in A1 of this dance will take a bit of practice to get right, but it's fun trying – some people never crack it!

Despite this dance being rather 'formal', children seem to love trying it out.

Beauty in Tears

16 bars: Twice through the dance = Once through the music

A1   Right hand turn your opposite, half round and then back to place with the left hand.
Promenade hold with your partner, two **chassee** steps left, two chassee steps right passing your opposites, move on to the new couple and with them make a right hand **star**, going half way round until you are facing the direction you originally came from.

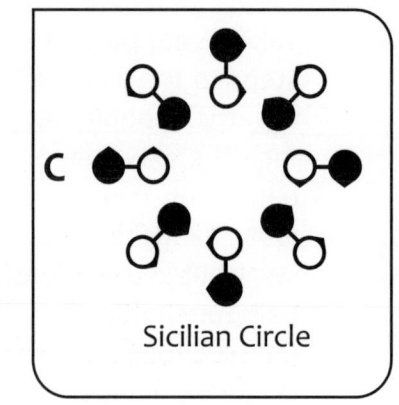

A2   With your partner two chassee steps left, two chassee steps right, pass back to your original couple and half left hand star to original places.
Waltz, passing your opposites on to next couple, the ones you have already met.

Sicilian Circle

CD 1/8: - The Kite / The Jewish Tune ~ 32 bars

Pawnbroker Roger Watson

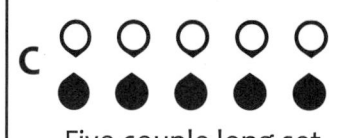

Couples number themselves 1, 2, 3, 4, 5 from the top of the set.

Five couple long set, that tells a story

A1   1s, holding inside hands, go down the middle of the set followed by the 2s. 2s make an arch and the 1s turn underneath back to their place followed by the 2s.

No 1 couple are in debt, they owe the 2s lots of money, so they go down the set hotly pursued by the 2s. The 2s foolishly make an arch and the 1s escape underneath it back to their place followed by the 2s.

A2   1s go down the set again followed by the 3s. 3s make an arch and the 1s turn underneath back to place, followed by the 3s.

But it's not just the 2s that they owe money to; it's the 3s as well. So off go the 1s down the set followed by the 3s this time. 3s also make the mistake of making an arch and the 1s escape underneath it back to their place followed by the 3s.

B1   The top two couples make a circle and the remaining ladies and the remaining men each make a circle and circle round to the left and back to the right to place.

Explain what a pawnbroker's shop is, and now make the sign of the pawnbroker's shop by making the three 'balls' as described above. Into the pawnbroker's shop (circle left) and back out again (circle right).

B2   No 1 couple stand in the middle of the set, whilst the other couples join hands around them, and move forward into the middle and back out again, booing, hissing and making comments such as 'Give us our money' etc. This couple move out of the middle of the set and join on the bottom end of the set ready to start the dance again with a new 1, 2, 3, 4, and 5.

Finally, still unable to pay their debt, the 1s are thrown into prison, with everyone booing and hissing around them. 1s escape out of prison, join the end of the set, ready to start all over again with another couple deeply in debt!

For your own notes

Foula Reel

Four couple long set

A1 & 2   Top couple face down the set, holding inside hands, and dance to the bottom.

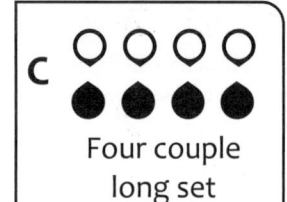

Strip the Willow back up the set.

B1   Again holding inside hands, the top couple make a **single arch**, man on the right, and go over the heads of the gentlemen, at the bottom of the set the lady twirls under his arm, enabling him to move to the outside of the ladies row, and then they arch over the heads of the ladies. She twirls again allowing the man to resume his position.

B2   All couples take their partners by both hands and pousette or push and pull as follows. Top man pushes his lady back four steps and then pulls her towards him four steps, at the same time they weave in and out of the other couples, making their way to other end of set. Couples 2, 3 and 4 pull and push in the same way, thus avoiding the top couple. The new top couple is ready to start again, facing down the set.

Tangledwood Jane Downes

Five couple long set

A1   Middle couple separate and each turn to their left, so that the man joins the top two couples in a circle and the woman joins the bottom two couples in a circle, circle left and then right.

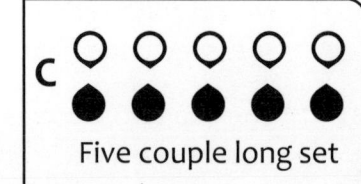

A2   The middle couple quickly swap ends and **star** right and left with the other couples.

B1 & 2   *Information – Be aware that the middle three couples will dance a Kentish Swing whilst the very end couples have other instructions to follow.*
Kentish Swing – middle couple right arm turn their partner half a turn and then the gentleman left arm turns the bottom lady of the three couples and his lady left arm turns the top man (of the three). The middle couple right arm turn each other again, and then the gentleman left arm turns the top lady and the lady left arm turns the bottom man.

Meanwhile couples 1 and 5 **do si do** by the right and then left shoulder, and right and left arm turn their partner or, alternatively, passing their partner by the right shoulder, they travel all the way round those dancing the Kentish Swing, until they return to their places, keeping up the pace of the dance.

Top couple of the five dance down the middle of the set, everyone **swinging** their partner as they pass. New middle couple get ready to start the dance by each turning to their left.

If you wanted to dance Tangledwood with less experienced dancers, you could leave out A2, giving more time for the Kentish Swing and the final part of the dance, including a slight breather! Similarly, for newcomers, older or very weary dancers, let couples 1 and 5 have a rest during the Kentish Swing.

> **CD 2/1: The Braes of Tollymet / Harry Cox's Schottische** ~ 32 bar schottisches. Dance to a **Step Hop.** Or use **CD 2/8**

Three Around Three aka Sheepskins

Although we have set this dance to a schottische, it can in fact be danced to any of our tunes.

A traditional 'game' dance for three people and a row of, originally, three hats or other items on the ground, to dance around. Space the hats out, say one or two metres apart.

The idea is that the first person leads the row of three in and out of the hats in an extended figure of eight and as that leader circles the third hat to return, the last person in the row circles the middle hat to become the new leader. The 'figure of eight' continues with the last person becoming the leader every time they come to the middle hat, until such time as everyone has had enough, or the music ends!

For a real brain teaser, opportunities for extending this dance into grid of nine are challenging.

Jane's Hornpipe Jane Downes

- A1 Trios, linking arms, dance four steps forward, four steps BACKWARDS and repeat.
- A2 Gentlemen right arm turn their right partner, left arm turn their left partner and then repeat.
- B1 Trios make right and then left hand **stars**.
- B2 Trios circle left and the two ladies pop the man forwards, under the arch of their joined hands, to the next ladies along, receiving their new partner from behind them.

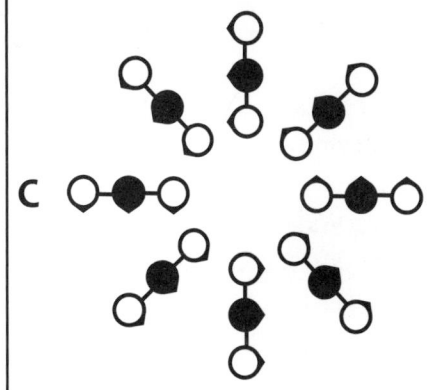

Trios following each other in a large circle facing anticlockwise. Gentlemen between two ladies.

Mock Turtle Dave Hunt

All the couples facing clockwise round the room are No 1s and those facing anticlockwise No 2s.

- A1 Join hands in groups of four, circle left and back to the right.
- A2 **Arches**, couples face each other holding inside hand with partner, 1s make a single arch over the 2s that they are facing, 2s make an arch and let the 1s come backwards underneath back to place, repeat.
- B1 In groups of four, right and then left hand **stars**.
- B2 **Promenade** hold, **chassee** four steps out to the right, back in and **swing** partner around.

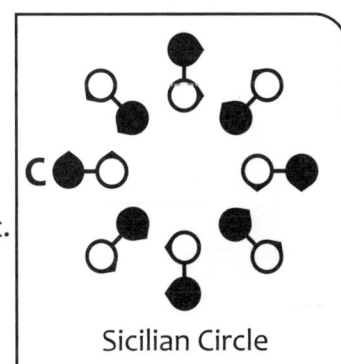

Sicilian Circle

Nottingham Swing

16 bars: Twice through the dance = Once through the music

Setting up explanation! Ask the top couple to turn and face down the set and the next couple to turn and face them and all four join hands. Continue this all the way down the set making sure there is an even number of couples. All the couples facing down the set are 1s and the others are 2s. Let go hands.

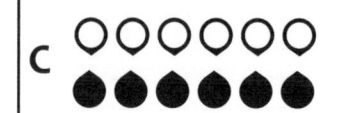

Long set all the way down the room for as many as fit in

Note: when setting this up with children it is best to walk down the set, physically numbering each couple 1, 2, 1, 2 etc but still ask them to join hands so that they know who they will be dancing with in the first instance.

A1 No 1 men and No 2 ladies right arm turn using up the full eight beats.
    No 2 men and No 1 ladies right arm turn.

A2 All the No 1 couples take both hands with their partner, take two side steps down the middle of the set and back again to their place. Letting go of their partner's hands, face up to the top of the set, turn away from each other casting round the No 2 couple they have just danced with, then come back together again. Everyone **swing** their partner. Beware of the whole set moving further and further away, encourage No 2s to take a slight step towards the caller.

To start the dance again the No 1 men turn to their right and right arm turn with a new No 2 lady. The No 2 men turn to their left and right arm turn with a new No 1 lady. During this time there will be a couple at either end of the set who have no one to dance with – they can just have a rest, but as everyone moves on through the dance they will find that there is another couple to dance with. HOWEVER after standing out at the top of the set, the couple that had been a No 2 now become a No 1 couple and the couple at the bottom of the set that started off as a No 1 couple now become No 2s. More simple than it sounds, the rule is have a rest and change your number!

Billy's Hornpipe   Eddie Upton

Couples numbered up 1, 2, 3, 4 from the top of the set.

Four couple long set

A1 No 1 man and the No 2 lady, No 3 man and the No 4 lady right arm turn and then left arm turn their partner.

A2 No 1 lady and the No 2 man, No 3 lady and the No 4 man right arm turn and then left arm turn their partner.

B1 **Hey** in your lines of four. No 1 man face away from the caller, No 2 man turn and face him. No 3 man face away from the caller, so that he is standing back to back with the No 2. No 4 turn and face the No 3. Starting by passing right shoulders, all the men weave in and out of each other, moving up and back down the line to places. Remember, when you get to the end of the line always come back in with the right shoulder.

Ladies do the same, simultaneously with the men.

B2 No 1 couple dance a stately **Promenade** down the middle. Everyone **swing** their partner around.

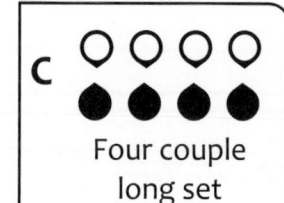

CD 2/2: La Ronde de la Millereine / Title Unknown ~ 32 bar jigs

Farmyard Square

Couples numbered 1, 2, 3, 4. See Glossary **Square Set.**

A1   All four couples join hands, circle left eight steps and then right, back to place.

A2   No 1 couple turn and face each other, go past each other, around the outside of the set and back to their places.

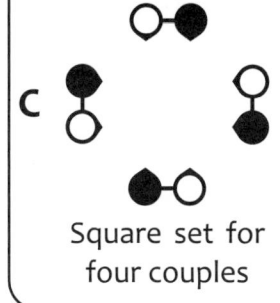

B1 & 2   Everyone turn and face their partners, and **Grand Chain** round the set back to place and **swing** partners.

The dance is repeated in the same way but the next time round it is the No 2 couple go round the outside of the set on A2, third time 3s, fourth time 4s. Then be inventive! Either repeat the same pattern again or ask the 1s and the 3s to go round the outside of the set at the same time, then the 2s and the 4s, even everyone! Great fun!

Square set for four couples

Mad Jack's Galop

All couples facing in clockwise direction are No 1s and the others are 2s.

A1   No 1s take partner in a **ballroom** or two handed hold and galop eight steps in the direction they were facing, between the other couples, and back to place, then step apart!

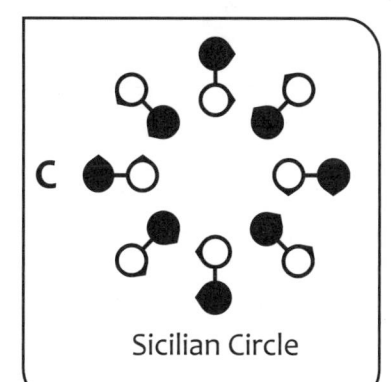

A2   Repeat A1 with 2s.

B1   1s and 2s face each other, right and then a left hand **star**, ensuring that you are back to your place.

B2   **Arches**, couples face each other holding inside hand with partner, 1s make a single arch over the 2s that they are facing, 2s make an arch and let the 1s come backwards underneath back to place. 1s arch over again but do not return, here is a new couple to dance with. 1s be ready to galop!

Sicilian Circle

Fee's Moulinex aka Yarmouth Long Dance

A1   Turn and face your partner; holding hands galop across the set to change places with your opposite numbers; if space is at a premium, think thin! Galop back to place.

A2   Right hand turn your opposite number and left arm turn your partner.

B1   Right and then left hand **star** in your fours.

B2   Top two couples join hands in a circle and spin to the bottom of the set.

Continuous long set made up of couple facing couple, gentlemen with their ladies on the right

The Rifleman

Traditionally danced with a **rant** step, to a polka, you could also try this dance to Polkas de l'Avayron, CD 1 Track 5, or The New Victory, CD 2 Track 5.

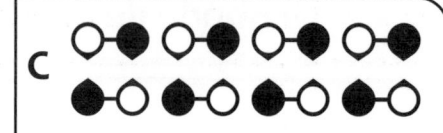

Continuous long set made up of couple facing couple, gentlemen with their ladies on the right

Top two couples join hands in a circle, then the next two couples, all the way down the set to establish that everyone knows who else is in their 'four'. Let go hands to return to starting positions.

A1   Hold hands along the line. Dance forward and back then the gentleman takes the lady opposite him back to his side, dancing her around to his left and putting her on his right hand side.

A2   Repeat the above, the gentleman taking his own lady back to his right hand side.

B1   **Ladies Chain** across the set and back.

B2   Top two couples dance to the bottom of the set. Everybody move up the room to make space for them at the bottom of the set.

King Offa's Delight, an easier version of Rifleman! Pat King

A1   Everyone hold hands along their line. Dance four steps forward and back again to place. The line to the right of the caller all raise their arms to make arches and the two sides swap over.

A2   Everyone hold hands again along their lines and repeat as above, with the line to the right of the caller making the arches.

B1   In groups of four, right and then left hand **star**.

B2   Be imaginative, let the top two couples work out their own plan for moving down the set! Everybody move up the room to make space for them at the bottom of the set.

This dance can be adapted for children in many ways; for instance the above variation can be altered so that instead of making a right and left hand star, the caller shouts out other instructions such as sit down, stand up, turn around, jump up and down – an excellent way of working on listening skills!

Another adaptation was to use this dance in a Harvest Festival with Special Needs children, this time just having two equal lines of dancers and not worrying about couples so that wheel chair users could be included.

A1   Everyone join hands along their line and sway backwards and forwards like corn in the wind, let go of hands and swap sides or turn around on the spot.

A2   Repeat A1.

B1   Right hand turn the person opposite, representing the rotary movement of the farmer cutting down the crops.

B2   Finally the top couple join hands and walk down the set together as if carrying home the harvest.

Note: Special Needs children and adults can easily cope with these dances, but each move may take 16 bars of music not the usual 8.

CD 2/3: News of the Victory / Woodland Flowers ~ 32 bar jigs

Triple Promenade aka Silly Threesome
Sibyl Clark

A bit of a game really! Gentlemen progress.

A1 Trios link arms and **promenade** along for the full eight bars.

A2 Gentlemen right arm turn their right partner, and left arm turn their left partner. Repeat.

B1 Join hands in a line of three to make double arches. The lady on the inside of the circle goes under the arch made by her partners with the man following through. Repeated by the outside lady.

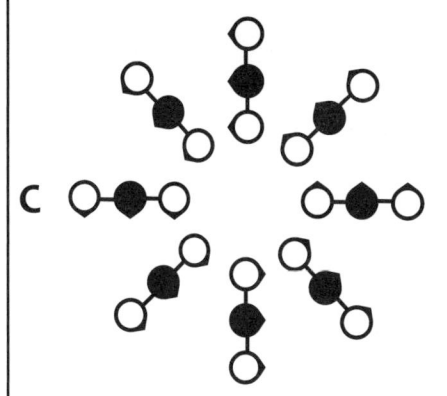

Trios following each other in a large circle facing anticlockwise. Gentlemen between two ladies.

B2 Ladies make a two handed arch forming a tunnel all the way round the room with the men moving through the tunnel until instructed to stop. This can either be done by the caller shouting 'Grab this one!' in plenty of time, or the music being stopped and the ladies grabbing the man that is passing them at the time. Any man left over, or pair of ladies without a man, go into the middle and grab whoever they need! Spare dancers can always hover in the middle of the circle from the start of the dance to join in the tunnelling and competition for partners.

When doing this with children, we usually start off by stopping the music at the end of B2, so that they get a chance to set themselves up in their trios before starting again.

Spitfire   Tony Dunn

Couples numbered up 1, 2, 3, 4 from the top of the set.

(This is another dance that can be used cross curricular, WWII.)

Four couple long set

A1 No 3 lady and No 1 man, and No 4 lady and No 2 man, right and left arm turn.

A2 No 1 lady and No 3 man, and No 2 lady and No 4 man, right and left arm turn.

This represents the pilots' scramble to the aircraft.

B1 1s and 2s, 3s and 4s make a right hand star then a left hand star.

Starting up the propellers.

B2 Top couple **Dip and Dive**. At the same time, as the tops pass, each couple **casts out** to the bottom of the set, under the arch made by the top couple and back up the set.

The flight.

Royal Standard   Keith Leech and Dave Roberts

(Named to celebrate the Old Town pub, Hastings)

- A1 Ladies right hand **star** and when back to place left arm turn their partner.
- A2 Men right hand star and when back to their place left arm turn their partner.
- B1 Everyone turn and face their partner and **Grand Chain.**
- B2 **Swing** your partner round then gentlemen hand their lady onto the next man to his right, and she's ready to right hand star.

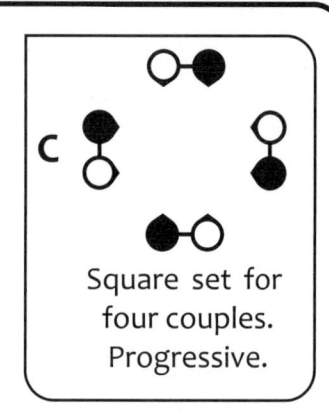

Square set for four couples. Progressive.

La Russe

64 bars: Once through the dance = Twice through the music.

Couples numbered 1, 2, 3, 4. See Glossary **Square Set.**

The person next to you is your partner, and the person on the other side is your corner.

- A1 Face your corner, **balance** twice and **do si do.**
- A2 Face your partner and repeat.
- B1 No 1 couple **swing.**
- B2 No 1 couple **promenade** around the set behind the number 2s, 3s and 4s back to place.
- A1 Everyone hold partner's inside hand. 1s and 3s swap sides, 1s making an arch and the 3s go underneath. 2s and 4s swap sides, the 2s making the arch. 1s and 3s cross back again, the 3s making an arch, and the 2s and 4s cross back again, the 4s making the arch.
- A2 Repeat until everyone is back in their original place. This isn't as difficult as it sounds, but needs to be practised a bit before the dance starts so that it flows smoothly.
- B1 All join hands, circle left, keep going using up the given music.
- B2 **Promenade** partners in anticlockwise direction back to place.

Square set for four couples

When everyone is completely at ease with the arches, have a bit of fun by changing the order!

Subsequent times through the dance, at the first B1, the second, third and fourth couples swing, promenade and may lead the arching.

Sea Captains

A1   All eight people join hands, circle left and right.

A2   Thread the Needle, see below.

B1   Dip and Dive, see below.

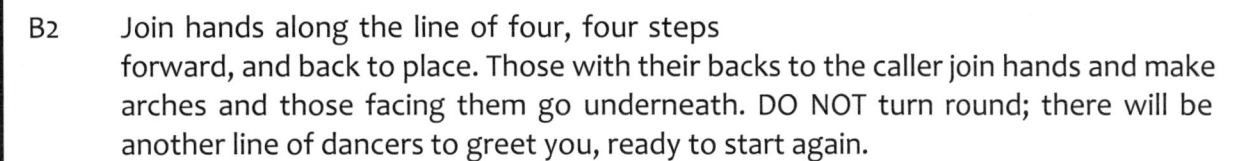

B2   Join hands along the line of four, four steps forward, and back to place. Those with their backs to the caller join hands and make arches and those facing them go underneath. DO NOT turn round; there will be another line of dancers to greet you, ready to start again.

Double Sicilian, in a straight set

BUT lines reaching either end of the room will find that they have no one to dance with; they turn round to face the other dancers, gentlemen swapping sides with their ladies so that their partner is again on their right hand side; they stand out of the next round of the dance, but get ready for the following one when there will be another line of four dancers to greet them.

Jargon Buster: Thread the Needle - keep holding hands, the right hand couple with their backs to the caller make a single arch. The gentleman opposite that couple does not hold hands with them but leads the other six under that arch, to return to their places, the arching couple staying still.

Jargon Buster: Dip and Dive (Double Sicilian circle style) - The plan is that the couples dance around the four sides of the rectangle which is their set, turning inward to meet each new couple, arching over and under alternately as they go. First to make arches are the couple who made the single arch for Thread the Needle and the diagonally opposite couple. They arch over their opposites and turning inwards, dive under the next couple's arch, over the next and under the last, back to place.

For your own notes

CD 2/4: - Horses Branle or Brawl ~ 48 bars

Farendole

A fourteenth-century line dance which allows leaders a free choice from a variety of possibilities.

All join hands in a long line:

- *Serpent* - the leader takes the line of dancers anywhere they wish, even in and out of doors, maybe even catching up with the last people in the row and through an arch made by them, and on again.

- *L'escargot* – the snail; the leader becomes the centre point of a tight spiral, by turning in with everyone closely following. With the spiral almost complete, the leader turns back on him/herself, unwinding the line. Alternatively, the leader can duck under any pair of hands and, drawing the line with him/her, unwind to proceed to another formation.

- *Rattlesnake Twist* – the leader turns under the arch made by themselves and their next-door neighbour and, letting go, continues to weave in and out of the line. That next-door neighbour then turns under the arch made by themselves and the next neighbour along, letting go hands and following their leader. Every member in the line will take their turn letting go hands and doing the Rattlesnake Twist. Eventually the leader will proceed to another formation.

- *Worm* – the first two people make a double arch. As everyone ducks under, the next two people make an arch and the next until you have a 'tunnel' of arches. The leader worms their way through the tunnel taking their partner, with everyone following out into a line again, or alternate dancers splitting off left and right to form two lines of farendole.

- *Caterpillar* – the leader becoming tired can at any point lean against a wall, making an arch through which the second person in the line takes the lead, dances away perhaps into a serpent, with the original leader joining on the end.

- There is always the option for a long line of dancers to be split by one who would become a leader.

- The farendole could draw to a close with the line becoming a circle, dancing into the middle and out. Children like to shout something appropriate like the name of their school/group.

A much simpler version which could be used by even very young children is for an adult leader to take the serpent where they will, through arches made by other helpers or even under a strategically placed table!

Midland Nine Pin

Information – This is a simple unphrased dance which can be added to or deconstructed at will.

The dance starts with head couples, ie those with their backs to and facing the caller, galoping across the circle, sides galop across, head and then side couples galop back again.

Followed by a selection from the following:

- All dance into the middle and out.

- All circle left and right.

- **Do si do** and **swing** partners.

- All **promenade.**

- Right and then left arm turn partner, then turn round and repeat with the person behind you.

- Face your partner and start a **Grand Chain** to the ninth person. Be inventive!

Circle dance

Horses Brawl Sothcott/Upton's happy combination of Horses/Montarde Branles (*Orchesography*) first danced in Southwark in 1970s

Number everyone in the set, No 1, the leader, being the person furthest round to the left. The eight join hands in an open circle.

A1 & 2   Led by that first person, everyone steps left foot to the left, then right foot behind the left, left foot next to the right and jump, 'side, behind, together, jump', eight times in all. The caller could encourage energetic dancing and height of jumping, or lead by example!

B1 & 2   Everyone let go hands. The leader now has two bars of music in which to twirl and dance across the gap in the set and stand by the last person, No 8. Each member in turn dances expressively across the gap until they all end up as started.

C1 & 2   The leader now goes into the middle of the set and weaves between 2 and 3 and back between 3 and 4, into the middle, weaves between 4 and 5 and back between 5 and 6, into the middle, then in between 6 and 7 and back between 7 and 8 into the middle and then joins the line as the new last member.

Dance starts again with the new leader!

Have fun, encourage the dancers in B1 & 2 to use their 2 bars of music inventively, some may even cartwheel, leapfrog and breakdance!

For those who find the jumping too energetic, the dance can be done in a gentler way, ie A1 step side, behind, together, bend knees or clap. Adapt this further for special needs or your youngest dancers who love to cheer!

A medieval three part French dance for eight people in an open circle (horseshoe shape)

CD 2/5:- The New Victory / Down the Road ~ 32 bar polkas

Dave Robert's Polka

16 bars: Twice through the dance = Once through the tune

A couple dance, place yourselves anywhere in the room, with a **ballroom hold** or similar.

A1   Four steps to the gentleman's left and four steps back again. He takes four more steps left whilst the lady twirls under his arm once. Ballroom hold and one quick **polka** round.

A2   Repeat as above, but to the gentleman's right.

Buttered Peas

Couple facing couple anywhere around the room.

This dance is similar to the next one, Scatter Polka, but has the advantage that partners will stay together, perhaps making it suitable for younger children.

Couple facing couple anywhere around the room.

A1   All four join hands and circle left, then back to the right.

A2   Right hand **star** and back with the left.

B1   Turning away from your partner to your opposite, do three right hand shakes, then clap your hands three times, three left hand shakes, clap your hands three times and quickly turn back to your partner to do the same with them.

B2   Gentlemen now dance their partners off in any direction and keep going until the caller shouts out 'STOP!' at which point they grab the nearest new couple. The art of the caller is to warn the dancers, just in time, that the music for the next dance through is on its way. People who don't quickly get another couple to dance with should wave their arms, attracting attention to themselves whilst searching.

For your own notes

Scatter Polka

A1 All four join hands and circle left, then back to the right.

A2 Right hand **star** and then a left.

B1 Gentlemen right arm turn their partner, then left arm turn the other lady.

B2 Gentlemen now dance this lady off in any direction and keep going until the caller shouts out 'STOP!' at which point they grab the nearest new couple. The art of the caller is to warn the dancers, just in time, that the music for the next dance through is on its way. People who don't quickly get another couple to dance with should wave their arms, attracting attention to themselves whilst searching.

Set a children's challenge with this dance – how many different people can they dance with?

> Couple facing couple anywhere around the room. Progressive.

Ranting Polka

Explanation! Ask the top couple to turn and face down the set and the next couple to turn and face them and all four join hands. Continue this all the way down the set making sure there are an even number of couples. All the couples facing down the set are 1s and the others are 2s. Let go hands.

> Continuous long set, gentlemen standing opposite their partner

Note: when setting this up with children it is best to walk down the set, physically numbering each couple 1, 2, 1, 2 etc but still ask them to join hands so that they know who they will be dancing with in the first instance.

A1 Circle of four hold hands, **rant** four times and circle left.

A2 The same four rant four times and circle right, making sure everyone is back to place.

B1 **Arches**, couples face each other holding inside hand with partner, 1s make a single arch over the 2s that they are facing, 2s make an arch and let the 1s come backwards underneath back to place, repeat.

B2 Take partner in a **ballroom hold** and **polka**, passing each other, using up the music and progressing to a new couple; be ready to start again. End couples in the set stand out and return to the dance next time round.

Remember, after standing out at the top of the set, the couple that had been a No 2 now become a No 1 couple and the couple at the bottom of the set who started off as a No 1 couple now become No 2s. More simple than it sounds, the rule is have a rest and change your number!

CD 2/6:- The Sweets of May / Dingles Regatta ~ 48 bar jigs

Sweets of May

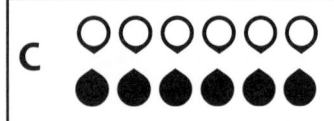

A1 Ladies join hands; top lady leads all the others around the back of her gentleman, down the outside of his row and back to place.

A2 Gentlemen repeat as above.

B1 **Jump and Kick** twice and **swing** your partner round once, leap apart!

B2 Top couple take both hands with their partner and galop down the set, then back up again.

C1 & 2 Top couple **Cast and Arch,** everyone swing their partner around.

Long set dance for 5 – 7 couples

Ninepins

Couples with their backs to the caller and facing the caller are head couples, the other two couples at the side of the set are side couples.

Our version of the popular dance. For this dance the piece of music will need to be stopped before the 48 bars are up and then started again for each round of the dance. Great fun for children and adults alike!

A1 Head couples take their partners by both hands and **galop** across the set (avoiding the ninepin, gentlemen could dance back to back across the set and ladies back to back on the return) and back again to place.

A2 Side couples do the same.

B1 Head couples join hands, circle left and right with the ninepin spinning and leaping in the middle.

B2 Side couples do the same.

C1 Assuming that the ninepin is a man he takes each lady in turn and dances her round once.

C2 All five men join hands in the middle of the set and circle left, continuing to do so until the music is stopped with the caller shouting out 'NINEPIN'! Each of the men then quickly makes a dive for one of the ladies, the remaining man becoming the new ninepin!

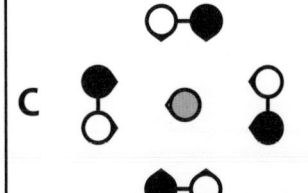

Square set with an extra dancer, the 'Ninepin', in the middle. Progressive.

Of course, if the ninepin is a lady, she dances each of the gentlemen around in turn as described above and then all the ladies circle left until 'Ninepin' is called, leaving one of the ladies in the middle.

With a mixed sex set of children for B2, the ninepin chooses a random partner from each side of the square to dance with. Then both the ninepin and those in the set who were not chosen make up the circle of five needed for C1 & 2.

Waves of Tory

Five couple long set

A1 Join hands down the line, and go forward four steps to meet each other and back again. Top two couples and the next two couples make a right hand **star** all the way round, back to place, with the fifth couple doing a right arm turn, or, later in the dance, taking a rest.

A2 Repeat A1 with left hand stars.

B1 Top couple take both hands with their partner and **galop** down the set and back up again.

B2 Top couple **Cast and Arch;** they are the 'archers'.

C1 & 2 The 'archers', now at the bottom of the set, face up the set ready to **Dip and Dive**, and all the other couples face them, holding inside hands. That bottom couple will go under the arch made by the next couple, make an arch themselves over the next, under and over and so on. This continuous section of the dance needs all the dancers, on reaching the ends of the set, to turn round and go under, dipping and diving themselves, until they reach their original places, with the 'archers' remaining at the bottom of the set.

Golden rule - at each end of the set, turn and go under.

*Experienced dancers might get a chance to **swing** their partner before restarting the dance.*

C1 & 2 May also be danced; coming under the arch to the top of the set the new top couple turn their backs on the caller and start the Dip and Dive from the top end continuing as usual. We like this!

Long Thady

Four couple long set

In the absence of a 2A, 3B piece of music, we have added an extra movement to the dance Thady U Gander, an all time favourite. Thady U Gander is Yorkshire dialect for 'follow my leader'.

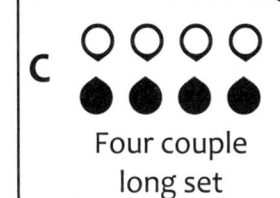

A1 Top two couples, and the next two couples, make right and left hand **stars**.

A2 Top couple holding inside hands dance down the set to the end, swap sides and go up the outside of the set to the top and stay on that opposite side.

B1 The top man leads his row of ladies round the back of his partner and the gentlemen's row back to place.

B2 The top lady similarly takes her row of men.

C1 & 2 Top couple **Strip the Willow** to end of set.

Pete's Needle Pete Collins

Couples numbered 1, 2, 3, 4. See Glossary **Square Set**.

This dance is not as difficult as it sounds.

Square set for four couples

A1 & 2   Double star, that is, gentlemen put their right arm round their lady's waist and make a left hand **star**. You may be able to dance twice round, but remember, the gentlemen have to let go of their star and move their ladies in so that they can return to places with a ladies right hand star in time for the...

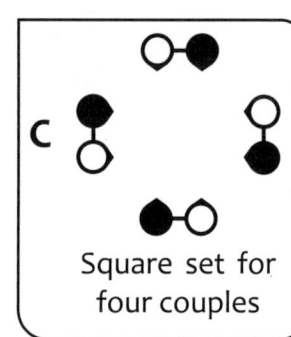

B1   ...No 1 couple to hold inside hands and make a **single arch**. All the other couples join hands in a semi circle. 1s take their arch over that semi circle, going over the 2s, 3s and 4s. At the same time the No 2 man leads the semi circle around under the moving arch twice, everyone returning to places.

B2   Join hands in a circle and dance into middle and out again twice.

C1 & 2   **Grand chain** and **swing**.

For your own notes

CD 2/7: - Terribus / The 42nd Highlanders' Farewell to Gibraltar ~ 32 bar marches

Pooey Nappy Polka Jane Downes

16 bars: Twice through the dance = Once through the music

No strict form, dancers take their partner anywhere on to the floor, facing away from the caller, gentleman with his lady on his right hand side.

A1 Hold partners inside hand, take four steps forward, let go partner's hand, turn around to face the caller, hold hands again then dance BACKWARDS four steps.
Four steps forward (towards the caller), let go hands again, turn round (with back to caller) and again dance BACKWARDS four steps.

A2 Turn and face your partner ready for some clapping. Clap your own hands together and under your right leg, then together and under your left leg, then together, behind you and three times quite quickly on your partner's hands. **Swing** your partner.

Gayish Gordons

16 bars: Twice through the dance = Once through the music.

A1 Gay Gordons hold, see below. Take four steps forward, turn and four steps BACKWARDS. Four steps forward, turn and four steps BACKWARDS.

A2 Gentleman hold his partner's inside hand, **'set'** together, apart and gentleman passes the lady across in front of him into his left hand, still facing anticlockwise. Holding inside hands again, 'set' together, apart and the lady turns under her partner's left arm and moves onto the outside of the gentleman behind who has his right arm ready to 'Gay Gordon's hold' her.

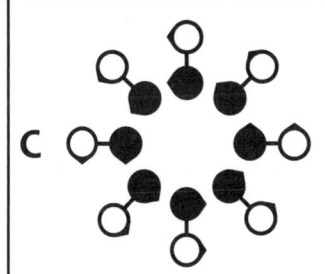

Couples in a large circle, all facing anticlockwise around the room, gentlemen on the inside. Make sure couples are well spaced out. Progressive.

Jargon Buster: Gay Gordon's hold, couple stand next to each other, gentleman with his lady on his right, the gentleman puts his right arm along his partner's back to her shoulder where they hold right hands. They join their left hands in front of them. In this way they can swivel round to face the opposite direction, simply by keeping hold and both turning to their right. The joined right hands drop in front as they turn, and the left hands come to the shoulder.

Six Meet   Pat Shaw

48 bars: Three times through the music = Twice through the dance. For this reason A1 often sets off really quickly and the dance will finish at a B2.

Trios with their backs to the caller and facing the caller are head trios, the other two trios at the side of the set are side trios.

A1 Head trios dance four forward and four back, forward again and the ladies swap to the other gentleman going BACKWARDS with him to his place.

A2 Side trios do the same.

B1 Heads trios repeat A1, ladies back to own man.

B2 Sides do the same.

A1 Gentleman right arm turns his right lady, and left to his left, and repeat.

A2 In trios join hands and circle left three times, ladies let go their joined hands and propel their gentlemen to the next pair of ladies to the right.

Square set of trios each with a gentleman in the middle. Spread out if possible. Progressive for the gentlemen.

The New Mrs Arrowsmith   Gordon Potts

See Glossary **Square Set**.

A1 Head couples step four forward and four back. Sides get ready a **single handed arch**. Going forward again the heads turn away from their partners, under that arch and back to places.

A2 Sides forward and back and do the same as above, with the heads making the arches.

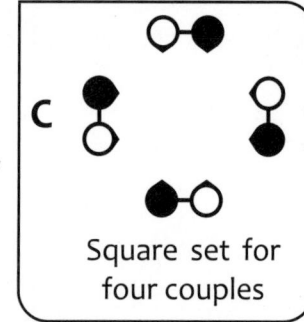

B1 & 2 *Information, this is almost like a Square **Strip the Willow** as in CD1 Track 3, the ladies making right hand **stars** and left arming their partner, but he keeps moving on round the set!*

*As the ladies make their first right hand **star**, all the gentlemen move on one place to the right, where their own lady will left arm turn them. The ladies go back into a right hand star and with the gentlemen moving on one more place to the right, they left arm them again. This sequence continues twice more, until everyone is back in their original spot.*

Square set for four couples

We like the following variation, ensuring that all dancers are kept on their toes!

A1 *No 1 couple only, forward and back and under the arches.*

A2 *No 2 couple as above.*

and second time through the dance A1, third couple make the moves and A2 the fourth couples. Third time through the dance could be as our notation above describes, and the fourth time, return to No 1 couple in A1 and No 2 couple in A2, with the gentlemen now making the right hand stars in B1 & 2 and the ladies moving on a place each time.

Glossary

Gentlemen always have their lady standing on their right unless otherwise stated.

Arches

- Single - Stand side by side with partner, hold nearest hand and lift to make an arch. This arch is often the best one to use when the couple are required to move and make an arch at the same time, eg arch over ladies in Boston Tea Party

- Double - Partners face each other, join hands and lift high to form an arch for others to go underneath. This arch is best used when standing still, very often after casting down the outside of a set as in Dance to Amelia's Birthday.

Balance or Jump and Kick

Facing your partner, both give a small jump, then kick your right leg across in front of your body, then jump again and kick your left leg across.

Ballroom Hold

With the couples facing each other, the man places his right hand around the lady's waist, the lady places her left hand on the gentleman's right upper arm, near the shoulder. They join their free hands, slightly extended at about shoulder height.

Basket

Two couples meet together, the gentlemen joining hands firmly behind the ladies' backs, and the ladies putting their hands loosely on the shoulder of the gentleman either side of them. The ladies should not hold each others hands along their partners' necks thereby causing strain. Everyone lean out and put their right foot in slightly and 'scoot' round to their left. In this fashion the ladies' feet may leave the ground as they are swung round by their pivoting partners; *Safety issue,* this is not obligatory!

Caller

The person who explains and walks through the dance with the dancers before the music starts and then continues to call instructions where necessary during the dance.

Cast

Couples face the top of the set, turn out away from each other and go down the outside of the set.

Cast and Arch

Top couple cast away from each other and down the outside, everyone following. The top couple make an arch at the bottom of the set, everyone else coming round the outside of them, underneath the arch and back up the set, maybe to swing their partner around. With children, suggest they follow their leader, and the leaders make an arch.

Chassee

A side step with your partner in ballroom or two handed hold.

Circle

All couples join hands to make a large circle, the gentlemen making sure that their lady partner is on their right.

Circle round (often circle right or left)

Join hands in a circle and dance around.

Corner

In a square set, your partner is on one side of you and your corner is on the other side.

Dip and Dive

One method is that the top couple turn towards the bottom of the set holding hands and all other couples turn towards the top of the set holding their partner's hand. Top couple go under the arch made by the second couple, arch over the third couple, under the fourth couple's arch, and so on until this couple reach the bottom of the set.

Another method could make the bottom couple leaders.

Dip and dive may also be a continuous, progressive movement as in Waves of Tory.

Do si do *aka* Back to Back

Partners face each other, take three steps forward passing right shoulders, a step to the right and then three steps back to their place without turning round.

Double Circle

An inner and outer circle, so that partners are facing each other.

Double Sicilian Circle

Two couples standing side by side in a line facing another two couples, gentlemen with their ladies on their right. Constraints of space usually mean that these lines of four will form a continuous set down the room.

Forward and back

Lines of dancers join hands and move forward a set number of steps and back again as a line.

Galop (from the French)

Holding hands with your partner or another dancer, side step in direction required.

Grand Chain (often found in circle or square set dances)

Couples turn and face their partner and give each other their right hand, dance past each other, let go hands and, without turning round, give their left hand to the next person that they face, move past and give right hand to the next dancer, and then their left hand. Continue in this way as directed for the dance. In basic terms dancers *all keep going in the direction that they originally face* giving right and left hand alternately to others as they meet them. This means that all the ladies are moving clockwise and the gentlemen anticlockwise.

Hey

A row of four dancers with the outside members facing in and the inside members back to back, facing the outsides. Dancers weave in and out of each other along the line and back to place, starting by passing right shoulders.

Irish Hold

Offer each other your right hands, with your forearms touching as if ready for arm wrestling. Comfortably place your left hand just above your partner's elbow and putting your right feet slightly towards each other, pivot, scooting round leaning away from each other. You can get quite a speed going on this, so hold tight!

Jump and Kick - see Balance

Ladies Chain

Ladies give their right hand to their opposite lady and, letting go, move onward towards the opposite man, putting her left hand into his. He puts his right arm around the back of her waist, 'wheels' her round forwards so that she ends up on his right hand side. Ladies give each other right hands again, and move to their own partners who will 'wheel' them round back to place.

Long set

A given number of couples make up a set standing facing each other in two straight lines eg four couple long set. Top or number one couple are the couple at end of the set nearest the music or caller, gentlemen to the right side of the caller, ladies to the left.

Open Circle

Dancers form a circle and then make one break, forming a horseshoe shape.

Polka

A 123 hop circling couple dance.

Progressive

Dances where couples separate and move on to a new partner. Be aware that children do not always appreciate this within mixed age dance groups.

Promenade

Walk side by side with your partner, simply holding nearest hands, or using a butterfly hold, that is, giving each other your right and left hands and walking in the desired direction; some call it a skaters hold.

Rant step

A step performed to a 123 rhythm. Jump lightly and land with right foot in front of left, hop on left foot at the same time lifting right foot, and finally another light hop on left foot bringing right foot down beside the left.

A common way to teach this step is to imagine that there is a fly on the floor and repeat the phrase 'squash that fly'; this gives the correct rhythm.

'Squash' – lightly stamping on the fly in front of your left foot to the first beat of music
'that' – hop on left foot (lifting right leg)
'fly' – another hop on left foot landing with both feet slightly apart.

Now repeat with the other foot!

Reel (in dance)

Line of three people standing slightly apart, the ends face in, the middle person turns to face one of those on the outside. Imagine a large figure of eight on the floor with the middle dancer standing at the point where the lines cross over; all three dancers move together in this figure of eight, passing right shoulders then left etc back to place.

Right arm/left arm turn

Partners face each other and give their right hand to each other - for a firmer grip move hand up to partner's elbow - and turn round, or left arm to each other, alternatively link inside of elbows.

Setting

Traditionally, especially in Scottish dances, 'setting' may be accompanied by using the hands held up, as antlers? A couple, facing each other, step simultaneously to the right and back to the left twice, lightly on the ball of the foot.

Sicilian Circle

Couple facing couple all the way round the room in a large circle (gentleman with his lady on his right).

Square set

Four couples making up the shape of a square, one couple with their back to the music/caller (head couple or number one couple), another couple facing them (also a head or number three couple) and a couple on either side (side couples). The couple to the right of the number ones are the twos and to the left of the number ones, the fours. In this formation all dancers are standing next to their partner; the person on the other side to the partner is the corner ie the corner of the square.

Square sets may also consist of trios instead of couples on each side of the set.

Star, right and left

Moving forward, couples join their right hands and dance round. Turning in they let go and join left hands to dance to back to place.

Step hop
We recommend you listen to schottische music to feel the basic step, hop, step, hop rhythm. You may encourage children to skip to that rhythm. (See also explanation for Schottische page 5)

Strip the Willow
Couple give each other their right arm and, first, go round one and a half times so that the man ends up on the ladies' side, and lady on the men's side, giving their left arm to that person on the outside of the set. Going round once, give your right arm back to your partner in the middle, go round once and then left arm out to the next person on the outside of set, gradually progressing up or down the set as the dance demands. The exception to this is Long Thady, where the starting couple have already swapped sides.

Swing
Take partner in a two hand hold, ballroom hold, waist hold or Irish hold and dance around on the spot.

Top couple/man/lady
Traditionally with a live band, the couple at the end of the set nearest the music, or the caller, depending on the layout of the room. In a long set the ladies have their right shoulder towards the top and the men their left.

Trio
Three dancers, usually a gentleman with two partners, one on either side.

Waist Hold
Face your partner with right shoulders touching, place your right arm across your partner's body to comfortably hold around their waist, left hand will clasp your partner's arm and off you go, scooting round.

Waltz
A couple dance circling round in a 3/4 time.

The **Catsfield Steamers** (www.catsfieldsteamers.co.uk) playing on the accompanying CDs are:

Andy Dennis ~ *Melodeon*

Will Downes ~ *Melodeon*

Paul Evans ~ *Drums*

Paul Roberts ~ *Banjo, Violin, Mandolin*

Roger Vance ~ *Banjo, Mandola*

Paul Dengate CD 2 Track 7 ~ *Guitar*

and

Edd Blakeley ~ *Guitar and Bass*

Recorded and Engineered by Edd Blakeley, **ejb studios**

Reproduced by SRT (www.soundrecordingtechnology.co.uk)

Faced with total beginners?

Try one of these suggested programmes:

Younger Children 5 - 8 yrs
Farendole ~ Page 36
Circassian Circle ~ Page 14
Midland Nine Pin ~ Page 37
Dance to Amelia's Birthday ~ Page 23
Sweets of May ~ Page 40
King Offa's Delight ~ Page 32
Pat-a-Cake Polka ~ Page 21

Older Children 8 - 12 yrs
Fee's Moulinex ~ Page 31
Horses Brawl ~ Page 37
King Offa's Delight ~ Page 32
Scatter Polka ~ Page 39
Farmyard Square ~ Page 31
Dance to Amelia's Birthday ~ Page 23
Muffin Man ~ Page 21
Ninepins ~ Page 40
Long Thady ~ Page 41
Children really seem to enjoy a continuous 'Strip the Willow', see page 17

Anyone 12 - 99 yrs
Oxo Reel ~ Page 14
Flying Scotsman ~ Page 12
Six Meet ~ Page 44
Muffin Man ~ Page 21
Fee's Moulinex ~ Page 31
Waves of Tory ~ Page 41
The Rozsa Waltz ~ Page 26
La Russe ~ Page 34
Then try a Strip the Willow, Long Thady ~ Page 41

Or experts?

Boston Tea Party ~ Page 16
Kerry Polka ~ Page 13
Nervous Breakdown ~ Page 16
Square Strip the Willow ~ Page 18
Willow Tree ~ Page 18
Malthouse ~ Page 20
Beauty in Tears ~ Page 26
Tangledwood ~ Page 28
Billy's Hornpipe ~ Page 30
Sea Captains ~ Page 35
The New Mrs Arrowsmith ~ Page 44

DANCE LIST alphabetical order

Beauty in Tears ~ CD 1/7 Page 26

Billy's Hornpipe ~ CD 2/1 Page 30

Boston Tea Party ~ CD 1/2 Page 16

Buttered Peas ~ CD 2/5 Page 38

Chip's Waltz ~ CD 1/7 Page 25

Circassian Circle ~ CD 1/2 Page 14

Circle Grab ~ CD 1/6 Page 23

Circle Waltz ~ CD 1/7 Page 25

Clopton Bridge ~ CD 1/4 Page 19

Country Bumpkin ~ CD 1/6 Page 24

Cumberland Square Eight ~ CD 1/5 Page 22

Dance to Amelia's Birthday ~ CD 1/6 Page 23

Dashing White Sergeant ~ CD 1/2 Page 15

Dave Robert's Dingle ~ CD 1/2 Page 15

Dave Robert's Polka ~ CD 2/5 Page 38

Drops of Brandy ~ CD 1/3 Page 17

Farendole ~ CD 2/4 Page 36

Farmyard Square ~ CD 2/2 Page 31

Fee's Moulinex ~ CD 2/2 Page 31

Florida Snowball ~ CD 1/3 Page 17

Flying Scotsman ~ CD 1/1 Page 12

Foula Reel ~ CD 1/8 Page 28

Gayish Gordons ~ CD 2/7 Page 43

Horses Brawl ~ CD 2/4 Page 37

Jane's Hornpipe ~ CD 2/1 Page 29

Kerry Polka ~ CD 1/1 Page 13

King Offa's Delight ~ CD 2/2 Page 32

La Russe ~ CD 2/3 Page 34

Long Thady ~ CD 2/6 Page 41

Lucky Seven ~ CD 1/6 Page 23

Mad Jack's Galop ~ CD 2/2 Page 31

Maggy's Square Set ~ CD 1/6 Page 24

Malthouse ~ CD 1/4 Page 20

Midland Nine Pin ~ CD 2/4 Page 37

Mock Turtle ~ CD 2/1 Page 29

Mon Reve Schottische ~ CD 1/4 Page 19

Monastery ~ CD 1/4 Page 19

Muffin Man ~ CD 1/5 Page 21

Nervous Breakdown ~ CD 1/2 Page 16

Ninepins ~ CD 2/6 Page 40

Nottingham Swing ~ CD 2/1 Page 30

Oxo Reel ~ CD 1/2 Page 14

Pat-a-Cake Polka ~ CD 1/5 Page 21

Pawnbroker ~ CD 1/8 Page 27

Pete's Needle ~ CD 2/6 Page 42

Pooey Nappy Polka ~ CD 2/7 Page 43

Ranting Polka ~ CD 2/5 Page 39

Royal Standard ~ CD 2/3 Page 34

Scatter Polka ~ CD 2/5 Page 39

Sea Captains ~ CD 2/3 Page 35

Six Meet ~ CD 2/7 Page 44

Spitfire ~ CD 2/3 Page 33

Square Strip the Willow ~ CD 1/3 Page 18

Sweets of May ~ CD 2/6 Page 40

Tangledwood ~ CD 1/8 Page 28

Thady U Gander, see Long Thady

The New Mrs Arrowsmith ~ CD 2/7 Page 44

The Rifleman ~ CD 2/2 Page 32

The Rozsa Waltz ~ CD 1/7 Page 26

The Tempest ~ CD 1/1 Page 12

Three Around Three ~ CD 2/1 Page 29

Triple Promenade ~ CD 2/3 Page 33

Waves of Tory ~ CD 2/6 Page 41

Willow Tree ~ CD 1/3 Page 18